Compliments of

INVESTMENTS

PEOPLE ARE
THE PRODUCT

A History of AIM

PEOPLE ARE THE PRODUCT

A History of AIM

AIM

FUNDS ®

MICKEY HERSKOWITZ
and IVY McLEMORE

Copyright © 2000 by Mickey Herskowitz and Ivy McLemore

All rights reserved. No part of this book may be reproduced or utilized
in any form or by any means, electronic or mechanical, including
photocopying, recording, or by any information storage or retrieval
system, without permission in writing from the Publisher.

Inquiries should be addressed to
AIM Funds
Corporate Communications Department
11 Greenway Plaza, Suite 100
Houston, Texas 77046

Library of Congress Cataloguing-in-Publication Data available upon request.

ISBN 0-9703311-0-X

VISIT US ON THE WORLD WIDE WEB
http://www.aimfunds.com

Printed in the United States of America
First Edition
DESIGN BY BRIDGETT AKIN, BRIDESIGN, INC.
PRINTED BY WETMORE PRINTING COMPANY

To the visionaries
who helped create one of
America's true success stories.
And to Sue and Julie, the best investments
the co-authors ever made.

Foreword

I can think of no more remarkable story in the fund industry than AIM. There was a window of opportunity over the last couple of decades to establish yourself as a major fund company, and AIM blasted right through it.

The neat thing about the story is that the company reflects a shrewd combination of being a start-up and very judicious acquisition, aided by brilliant marketing and distribution. Dozens of other fund companies had the same opportunity, but I can't think of any which executed it as well as AIM.

If you look at the way the firm was positioned in the '80s, AIM's story is even more impressive. Essentially, AIM was a bond shop that had pulled together a handful of equity funds – most notably the Weingarten, Constellation, and Charter Funds. The acquisition of the CIGNA funds in 1992 was another of several building blocks that really showed a vision.

AIM was not in the catbird's seat in the '80s. At that time, the company was still associated to a degree with high-yield bonds and fixed-income in general. It was also a load shop when supposedly the whole world was going no-load. It's a company that focused on performance and distribution and diversified its lineup in a very prudent and intelligent fashion.

What was most remarkable is that AIM's success wasn't a one-note sort of thing. It was doing a lot of things right. I've seen a lot of organizations that have done one thing right and had great success – such as Vanguard with indexing, and Janus with growth stocks. But in creating distribution and service and a diversified product line, AIM executed brilliantly.

When people write about the mutual fund industry, they notice good performance, and they notice assets going in, but they don't necessarily notice the service. If you're a rep selling funds, however, service means the world to you. If you mess that up, it's your reputation. And AIM did exceptionally well in terms of quality service. They've really hit on all cylinders.

Ted Bauer, Bob Graham, and Gary Crum have not been highly visible in the public eye. But if you ask anybody in the mutual fund industry who they most admire, those are the names that come up. It's not a public-relations war they've fought over the years, but they've done the right things.

DON PHILLIPS
CEO/MORNINGSTAR, INC.

Acknowledgments

Every book is a collaboration, the product of collective thought and passion and memory. Debts are owed to many in the preparation of this candid and informal history of AIM Management Group.

Research and outlines provided by Clara Caldwell and Dian Vujovich were invaluable. Many key players among management were generous with their time and recollections. We thank them as a group, aware that the reader will find their names in these pages.

Don Phillips, a University of Texas graduate who has risen through the ranks of the fund industry to become chief executive officer of Morningstar, Inc., was gracious enough to contribute the foreword.

Our gratitude also goes to those behind the scenes who assisted with the organization and production of the finished product. Members of AIM's Corporate Communications Department – Stephen Graddy, David Matheson, Neely Owens, John Roehm, and Catherine Tramuto – sorted through and helped obtain many photos, in addition to performing many deadline-related tasks.

Norman Woodson, manager of AIM's Communication Resources Department, and fellow staffers Nancy Clement, Paula Hammon, Norma Marfoglia, and Pauline Younkin were instrumental in the production process. Mary Kay

Coleman, manager of AIM's Marketing Communications Department, administrative coordinator Ruth Ellen Huebner, and Christi Dunn assisted with various phases of the project.

AIM's Bill Hoppe, Linda Julian, Steve Kahn, Pat Hamill May, Miriam Peterson, Kathy Pflueger, and Karla Siemens helped obtain or provide photos along the way, as did Anita Fiorello of Arnold Saks Design, Andrea Montgomery, Mark Montgomery, Becky Cemo, and the Roxbury Latin School. Work by photographers Steve Chenn, Jim Dumas, F. Carter Smith, Jeff Smith, and King Chou Wong also grace these pages.

Martha Foster allowed us liberal access to AIM's literature archives. David Bachert of AIM's Institutional Marketing Department, Pam Stephens and Chrystal Williams of Retail Marketing, and Patricia Lewis of The AIM Foundation each contributed content. Bridgett Akin of BriDesign did a superb job in designing the dust jacket and every page of the book. Earl McLemore, who has served as a proofreader for the co-authors at one time or another for almost a half century, once again helped us set the record straight.

Stephen Winer, David Kite, Carol Relihan, and Jim Anderson of AIM's Legal and Compliance Department navigated the fine points. The co-authors also extend their gratitude to Becky Andrews, Carol Drawe, Patti Hefley, and Frannie Reed for their many various contributions.

A special salute goes to AIM director of corporate resources Judy Creel, whose advice and keen insight helped nurture the project from conception to completion.

And, finally, sincere thanks to Ted Bauer, Bob Graham, and Gary Crum for their many efforts along the way.

MICKEY HERSKOWITZ
IVY MCLEMORE

Contents

"For every forward-looking man,
there are a thousand self-appointed defenders of the past."

TED BAUER

Bob Graham, Gary Crum, and Ted Bauer often were all dressed up, but uncertain where AIM's fortunes would take them.

Chapter One

STARVATION IS
UNACCEPTABLE

AIM wasn't an overnight success and didn't expect to be. The company made it the old fashioned way, with discipline, persistence, sacrifice, and grit. Its short-term goal was survival. Its long-term goal was to create a reasonable living for its employees. The firm staked its reputation on its ability to offer quality investment products and services that would provide value to shareholders while maintaining the highest levels of honesty and integrity.

No one had any idea just how many twists and turns AIM's remarkable story would eventually take when Ted Bauer invited a few guests to join him poolside in his backyard on a spring day in 1976. Bauer recently had left his position as director and chief investment officer at American General Insurance Company and president of its subsidiary, American General Capital Management, where he had been responsible for the first closed-end bond fund listed on the New York Stock Exchange. The

Houston-based insurance giant had undergone a change at the top, and Bauer's freedom had been squeezed.

Bauer's guests that day included Bob Graham and Gary Crum, boyhood friends who had played on the same Little League team – the Senators – in the fifth grade. Graham played second base and Crum played first, showing they could form a successful combination years before their business careers.

Graham and Crum were secure, but restless. Bauer had hired Crum out of graduate school, at The University of Texas. Crum's father was the director of the mutual fund subsidiary of American General, and a close friend of Bauer's. Crum asked Bauer to interview Graham for an open position and suggested that Bauer hire him approximately one year after graduate school.

Bauer had received offers from other companies when he left American General, but one of his goals was to work for himself. He and his wife, Ruth, sat in their Houston home and pondered their future. They considered returning to Baltimore, where Ted was well-connected. They met there and were married before Ruth moved to Houston. "Ted was 57. That's unemployable today," Ruth said. "I asked him, 'Why don't you take a vacation?' And he said, 'When you're just lying around on the beach, you start to smell.' So we sat in the kitchen and thought, 'What are we going to do?'"

Then Crum called. "There had been a good-bye party for Ted at Tony's Wine Cellar," Crum said, "and I remember everyone had a lot of fun and nobody wanted him to leave. We were all good friends. We had put together a good organization and it was a shame to see it just go down the drain. I asked him, 'How would you feel about

*During AIM's early years in a modest office on the 10th floor of the
Dresser Tower in downtown Houston, Ted Bauer's primary concern
was keeping the door open for business.*

our trying to put something together?' Then he said, 'Well, you ought to come over and let's talk about it.'"

They huddled around the Bauers' pool that day and continued the talks over lunch at an elegant Houston restaurant, The Brownstone. They drove out to a house on Galveston Bay, owned by the Crums, to crunch the numbers. A white paper was developed that projected best-, worst-, and middle-case scenarios for the proposed company over the first three years.

Soon, a very lean, almost modest plan began to take shape. They projected that in five years, the new company could have as much as $500 million under management. At that point, they thought they would have it made. For now, though, they were thinking in terms of baby steps.

Under the terms of his contract with American General, Bauer could hire only one of their employees a month for five months. Crum, who had managed $450 million in assets in a fixed-income portfolio, went first. Graham, who had responsibility for $300 million in fixed-income and equity private placements, was next to join. Both men were still in their late 20s, some 30 years younger than Bauer, but there was no generation gap. They bridged the years with trust and affection and confidence, each in the other. Their natures were a perfect blend. Bauer was the visionary. Crum was persistent, private, and caring. Graham focused on details.

Of the three, Bauer clearly had the most to lose. He was tall, 6-foot-3, white-haired, and patrician. He learned confidence and independence at an early age. His mother, a social worker, placed a strong emphasis on her son's education. Bauer was a graduate, and now a trustee, of the prestigious Roxbury Latin School, founded in 1645. He

AIM's original white paper as conceived in 1976.

was captain of the Roxbury football team, had set high school track records in New England, graduated from Harvard, and later received his MBA in business from New York University.

One week after graduating from Harvard, Bauer entered the Navy and served three years as a pilot over Africa and England. Although his father was a well-known cardiologist who eventually became president and chairman of the American Medical Association, Bauer developed an interest in finance. After the war, he went to work as an analyst on Wall Street for $2,200 a year. "They had a cafeteria and you got free lunches," he said. "That was important then." His salary went up in pennies. "One year they gave me a raise of $3 a week. I told them my commuting costs had gone up more than that."

He moved on to the First National Bank in New York, which ultimately merged with National City Bank, and then to U. S. Fidelity & Guaranty in Baltimore. By the early 1960s, he had worked his way onto a special payroll, one of nine – out of 7,500 employees – earning $25,000 a year. "As a result of that background," says Bauer, "I've known how tough it was in the workplace. I've always been a nut and a pain, fighting for people to get a better break, and not have to go through so much nonsense. I made myself unpopular. I was probably the worst corporate employee ever because I kept fighting the system."

The system didn't roll over and quit, but it suffered a bruise or two. Then came Bauer's mid-life career change, and culture shock, with the move to Houston in 1969 as chief investment officer and director of American General Insurance Company. "When I came to this town," he says, "the city had seven and a half million square feet of office space, and that much again under construction. At its peak in the early '80s, they had built 150 million square feet. I could sit here, where my office is now in Greenway Plaza, and look out my window and see 90 percent of the building cranes in America. It was incredible. You had to see it to believe how aggressive a town this was."

While the rest of the industry was sagging, Bauer helped take American General's mutual fund assets from a few hundred million to $1.7 billion by 1975. Then the run was over. But even at a time when most people would have been thinking about retirement instead of their next professional challenge, leaving American General proved to be the best move Bauer ever made.

"Sometimes, you just have to move on," Bauer says. "When you're still young and desperate and starvation is unacceptable, you go where the action is. You go where you can make it.

"Right after leaving American General, I was visiting Baltimore and one of the partners of a major investment bank asked if I was bitter. I said, 'No one wants to be around a bitter old man.' Those are words to live by. Bitterness doesn't do anything for you. It's a worm in your soul."

Bauer first sketched the idea for AIM on a doily while visiting with business associate Richard Timberlake at the Investment Company Institute's annual general membership meeting in May 1976. Originally, the company had three goals: to provide fixed-income management for pension funds and other institutional clients, to manage money for high net worth individuals with accounts of at least $100,000 and – when strategic opportunities presented themselves – to buy mutual funds.

FINANCIAL TREND
The Newsweekly of Southwestern Industry and Investments

Bauer's Company Eyes Mutuals

The management group for American International Management's Houston-based investment operations includes these six shareholder-officers: William D. Murphy, CPA and former senior accountant for a national accounting firm, who had broad responsibility for treasury, accounting and data processing for a major investment advisor; W. Thomas Fiquet, formerly executive vice president of Variable Annuity Life Insurance Co.; Charles T. Bauer; Gary T. Crum, who previously managed $450 million in mutual fund corporate bond portfolios; Stephen H. Pouns, specialist in analytical and fundamental credit research for fixed-income securities, and Robert H. Graham, who formerly had responsibility for $300 million in fixed-income and equity private placements for an insurance company.

| MURPHY | FIQUET | BAUER |
| CRUM | POUNS | GRAHAM |

AIM first made headlines by entering fixed-income asset management.

Bauer's greatest assets aside from his in-depth knowledge of the financial industry were his integrity and his ability to form strong relationships. Because of his reputation, friendships, and numerous industry contacts, he was able to enlist other talented individuals with diverse experience and backgrounds to help him launch a new endeavor.

Crum was the first to join. He had started his career as a financial analyst at American General. Graham was next. His degree was in electrical engineering, but he felt he also needed an education in finance. So he finished grad school at UT with two degrees – a master's degree in electrical engineering and an MBA. "I got into finance and investment courses and found out I liked them better than engineering," Graham says. "When I got out of business school, I wanted to try to find something that would combine the two. So I left business school without a job."

In the spring of 1973, Graham had called Crum to see if there were possibilities at American General. There weren't. Graham looked elsewhere and landed a job in the trust investment area of the Bank of the Southwest, where he started doing spreadsheets by hand in a windowless room. He had been on the job for three weeks when Crum called to say there was a position open at American General assisting the man who ran a private placement portfolio. About a year later, Graham began managing the Venture Fund, which American General had acquired from Channing.

"I quickly proved I was not a portfolio manager," Graham recalls. "But that's one of the reasons Ted is a remarkable person. He had loyalty from the people at American General because he would give young people a lot of responsibility and would show confidence in them."

Among AIM's other early hires were Tom Fiquet, formerly executive vice president of Variable Annuity Life Insurance Company; Bill Murphy, a former senior accountant for a national accounting firm; and Stephen Pouns, a specialist in analytical and fundamental credit research in fixed-income securities.

The company was incorporated on August 4, 1976, as American International Management. Ted Bauer presided over the meeting. Ruth Bauer and a neighbor, Dewuse Guyton, Jr., sat in as proxies for Mandy Moross and a group of overseas investors. The goal had been to obtain $600,000 in operating capital from the sale of stock, and $3.4 million in letters of credit. They missed their goal by $100,000 in cash and $1.3 million in credit. Bauer, acting as chairman, announced that the company had been incorporated by his purchase of 4,000 shares of its common stock at $1 per share.

Moross, whom Bauer had met during his days at American General, headed a group that had an original stake in American International Management. Moross eventually was elected chairman of the board and would serve in that position for 17 years. On the Houston side, the heavy hitters were French Peterson and Carey Crutcher. As president and chief executive officer, Bauer headed up a management team that, in addition to Crum and Graham, included Pouns as research analyst, Murphy as treasurer, Fiquet as sales manager, and Jayne James as secretary.

From the outset, Bauer determined that AIM would specialize in fixed-income management because that was his management team's primary strength. "You have to identify what you are," he says. "You can't be all things to all people. We had a unique expertise in the field of fixed-income investments, and we tried to sell that expertise to pension funds."

It's not always easy to decide what to name a company that harbors all of your hopes and dreams. The founders had chosen the name American International Management because it reflected diversity. But the name eventually exposed them to the threat of a lawsuit by American International Group, a huge New York insurance conglomerate which had clout in the form of a net worth of $4 billion. To avoid a legal battle they could ill afford, the founders quickly removed the periods and settled on AIM in late 1977.

At about the same time, OppenheimerFunds asked the company not to use "AIM" in the name of any of its funds because Oppenheimer had a fund called Oppenheimer AIM Fund, with the acronym "AIM" standing for "Aggressive Investment Management." Oppenheimer later changed the name of its AIM fund to Oppenheimer Global Fund, thereby abandoning its exclusive rights to the use of "AIM" in mutual funds.

Once the founders decided on the name "AIM," the new company was in need of a logo. That's when Graham called graphic designer Jack Amuny to come up with a catchy design. Graham had met Amuny during frequent pickup basketball games at St. John's High School and the YMCA. Within a matter of days, Amuny presented a sketch that has served as the company's logo for almost a quarter century. "All I tried to do was design a visual by taking the 'A' out of the name 'AIM' and make it look like multiple 'A's' because of the scope of their business," Amuny said. "I also wanted to have it look like an arrowhead that was moving."

Ted Bauer and Gary Crum first established an office at the Marathon Building in downtown Houston in 1976. AIM opened for business with only a card table, two chairs, a coffeepot, and a telephone that didn't always work.

While AIM was gaining a corporate identity, employees were still getting their feet on the ground. In the early days, everyone pitched in to handle the most mundane tasks. For example, Ruth Bauer remembers stuffing envelopes at AIM's first warehouse – her dining room table. She also recalls being heavily involved in entertaining possible financial backers and potential clients as well as the in-house staff. "When you didn't have a lot of money, you got a huge platter and filled it with baked chicken and made the presentation look really outstanding," she says.

Literally, from Day One, the launch was an adventure. The company first opened a temporary office in the

Marathon Building with a card table, two chairs, a coffeepot, and a telephone that didn't always work. Two months later, AIM took five rooms across the street in Dresser Tower, at 601 Jefferson in downtown Houston.

To make the company look substantial, pillars were placed outside the office and the name "American International Management" was put on the front door. Crum, whose grandfather's hobbies had inspired him to study architecture and drafting, bought and assembled do-it-yourself steel furniture for the company. And in a vignette that typifies the company's early struggles, AIM even came across a fine, solid mahogany conference table the founders had to move themselves.

Bill Montgomery, who was AIM's contact at First City National Bank and would eventually join the company for a short time, offered them the table at a bargain price when the bank decided to redecorate. A meeting was in progress when Bauer and Crum walked into the room to examine their prize. "We just waltzed in, looked at the table, and took it right in front of everyone," Crum said.

Getting the table out of the bank proved to be the easy part of the move. Since the table was an eight-foot long, solid block of wood, it wouldn't fit into the Dresser Tower elevator. They had to negotiate with the building's manager to have someone from Otis Elevator oversee the job, putting the table not inside the elevator but on top of it, then raise it to the 10th floor.

"A lot of the early days are just a blur," Graham says. "We were busy working on a lot of things, mundane things. We had three open houses and several cocktail parties. We needed a brochure and had to have a photograph taken. Our offices were pretty desolate. Goldman

Sachs was in our building, and we had some friends there. So we went up to their floor and borrowed their front door to have our pictures taken."

In the early days of AIM, the lean, struggling, difficult stage, determination kept the company afloat with Bauer's constant refrain, "Starvation is unacceptable." For most of 1976, they made phone calls, knocked on doors, and sometimes stared at each other and wondered how they could justify their paychecks. "I hate to look back and think how miniscule our chances of success were," Graham recalls.

Bauer readily admits those first years were extremely difficult for the company. "Manfred Gorvy, who was one of our backers in Europe, was a chartered accountant and not a laughing boy," Bauer says. "Every time he came to town, he would say, 'I think we'll have to shut you down.' I said, 'You can't shut us down, we've got your money and you won't get it back.' Then I would take him to the opera, or something of that sort, calm him down, and send him home."

Failure isn't final until you accept it. And starvation was still not acceptable. Crum recalls wearing out a lot of shoe leather traveling with Bauer on presentations to potential clients. Being short on staff, Crum would conduct all of his own research, write and prepare the proposals and accompanying collateral pieces, and assist with the actual presentation. Although the private account management sector of the company never took off, the few accounts they managed to garner went a long way toward paying the bills. Among AIM's early institutional clients were World Bank and Delta Airlines.

Initially, Graham was asked to oversee AIM's individual account management area. But when it failed to develop

American International Management Inc.

The Officers of the
American International Management Companies

Charles T. Bauer	M. D. Moross
Gary T. Crum	Robert H. Graham
W. Thomas Fiquet	William D. Murphy
Stephen H. Pouns	

are pleased to announce the opening of their offices
1080 Dresser Tower 601 Jefferson Houston, Texas 77002
(713) 654-0640

Specialists in fixed income portfolio management.

AIM trumpeted its move from its cramped, temporary headquarters in the Marathon Building to a spacious five-room office in the Dresser Tower.

and treasurer and compliance officer Bill Murphy left the firm, Graham took over to continue the building of the compliance structure that Murphy had started. "About the summer of 1977, I was beginning to wonder what I was going to do to justify my existence," Graham says. "So I stepped into the void left by Bill and became an expert on the Investment Company Act of 1940 and the rules and regulations pertaining to mutual funds."

During AIM's early years, Graham became absorbed in trying to untangle a legal mess the company had fallen into based on an investment tip by French Peterson, who was involved in a coal investment and also owned a natural gas processing plant. Peterson claimed to have the expertise to develop the coal business and promised AIM an income of $10,000 per month if it would act as general partner in J&J Coal Mining Partnerships, a position that required a degree of capital. AIM agreed, but within a year learned that there was no expertise. Worse yet, the coal mine was virtually worthless.

It took about one year for the coal fiasco to unravel and about another eight years to get it off the books. Over the years, Graham made frequent trips to Morgantown, West Virginia, where the mines were located. "The coal business made me a lot more careful and cautious going forward," Graham said.

Another difficulty arose when one of AIM's original investors backed out. Carey Crutcher had inherited a sizable fortune of $30 million and the business that later became Crutcher Resources. He gave AIM $5 million to manage and was on the books as a potential investor for another $1.275 million. A fearless risk-taker, Crutcher began to draw on his inheritance in a nearly single-handed effort to remake the agricultural system of Australia.

"That project was so big, and consuming money so fast, that our little ol' $5 million account was snatched up and gone in six months," Crum says. When Crutcher withdrew his financial commitment, AIM had to re-purchase the stock, all but $25,000 worth, and seek to replace the loan guarantee. AIM had been in business less than a year, "And we still weren't sure what we had," Crum recalls.

As is the case with most entrepreneurial companies, the unwritten rule at AIM was to do whatever it took to get the job done. To help the cause, Ruth had taken a cram course to become registered as a sales rep to help push AIM's money market funds. But Ruth soon learned she was facing an uphill climb. "Few people knew what a money market was," she explained. "Interest rates were between 12 and 16 percent. If I called someone and said, 'You've got $20,000 sitting in a savings account and you're getting 3 percent on your money, how would you like to get 16?' They would say, 'Aw, come on...how can you do that?'"

While their baby son, Douglas, was at day care, Ruth proved to be a secret weapon, working out of her kitchen. Mainly, she called on small businesses, posing as an executive secretary. "I would tell the operator some fictitious story," she said, "that I needed to mail something to the chairman of the company and I didn't have the correct spelling of his name. Then I'd hang up, wait for a while, and call back." Most times, using her crisp, professional voice she had developed as an employee with Legg Mason, she would get through. "Then if I got a secretary who was really stubborn, I'd wait a day or two and then call back with a different pitch. Of course, only one out of 30 would even bite."

But Ruth's perseverance eventually paid off. With her protective husband tagging along, but maintaining a discreet silence, she met a prospective client for lunch. Later, the shirt-sleeved investor called and said, "Ruth, come in and see me tomorrow. I've got $300,000 I'm going to put in the fund. I know you're a little anxious because you want this fund to work out. And I want you to know I've read everything about the fund and it's fine.

"But I do have one suggestion. The next time you go on a call, don't take that stiff in the blue suit with you."

Chapter Two

A BRAVE, NEW WORLD

One of AIM's original goals was to buy or organize a mutual fund, and a lot of effort went into finding funds that were for sale. The first attempt to buy a fund involved a closed-end bond fund. At least five other attempts followed, but all failed. "We found out quickly that no matter what your reputation is in the business, nobody would sell to you unless your company had a record," Bauer recalls.

By early 1977, AIM already had gone through its cash. Bauer told AIM's small group of employees that the company couldn't expect to get another dime of capital until the company turned a profit. "I wouldn't even let them paint the office walls," he said.

AIM went down many different roads looking for deals that would enable the fledgling company to survive. The revenue from AIM's few private accounts was barely enough to keep the doors open. Graham remembers that AIM's first attempt at private placement involved trying to raise capital for a local venture that specialized in shredding automobile tires. "This guy thought he had this great idea and he kept talking to Ted about it, but it was evident that we didn't have the contacts to raise money and private placement wasn't going to be a real contributor to our business," Graham says. "That's when we decided to concentrate on mutual funds."

Bauer was keenly aware of how difficult buying a mutual fund or group of funds could be. He had been flirting with the mutual fund business since 1962, when he was running the equity business for U.S. Fidelity & Guaranty Insurance in Baltimore. He was a close friend with Jack Stephens, who was based in Little Rock and later would serve as president of one of golf's grandest events, The Masters. "Jack and I got together in '62 and we flew to Kansas City to see the United Funds," Bauer recalled. "They were up for grabs and Jack thought they could be purchased for $32 million. But I couldn't persuade the people at USF&G to buy it. They were strictly insurance guys."

By today's standards, the mutual fund industry was a fledgling operation in the mid-1970s. Sales of the entire industry, excluding money market funds, was only $4.3 billion in 1976. Total assets were only $48 billion, and the number of shareholder accounts was approximately 8.9 million. The industry was completing its fifth straight year of net redemptions and the sixth year of decline in shareholder accounts. In short, the industry was small and getting smaller.

Nevertheless, AIM's founders believed the mutual fund industry was on the cusp of a growth spurt, and they would be proven right. By 1999, the industry would have $6.5 trillion in assets, partly as a result of the Baby Boom

Gary Crum enlisted Michael Milken's support in 1977 for High Yield Securities, the industry's first underwritten high-yield bond fund.

generation's insatiable appetite for mutual funds. AIM would be on the cutting edge of that growth, with $125 billion in net assets and 6.3 million shareholder accounts. Says Crum, "We've always said through the years that we may not have done everything right, but the one thing we did do is pick the right industry."

But with time and money running out in mid-1977, AIM had a desperate need for a breakthrough in its quest for a mutual fund and got one from an unlikely source – Michael Milken. A few years later, Milken would be known as the most powerful man on Wall Street. He also would become a controversial figure for his role in disruptive hostile takeovers that resulted in a guilty plea for violations of federal securities laws. Even Milken's detractors, however, can't dispute his reputation as a financial genius. And to this day, AIM's founders remain grateful for his help when it was needed at a crucial time.

In 1977, active management of bond portfolios was a relatively new idea engendered by the instability of interest rates in the early 1970s. About this same time, high-yield bonds were starting to gain attention within the securities industry. In fact, junk bonds came to be known as high-yield bonds during AIM's first fund offering when the company received permission from the SEC to use the term. In those days, only an elite number of portfolio managers had the reputation of being active managers of high-yield bond funds, and Gary Crum was one of them.

For many years, bond prices hadn't moved upward or downward because interest rates had been relatively stable during the 1960s. Then in the 1970s, when interest rates spiked upward, the value of bond portfolios plummeted. People started to take a second look at investments they once considered secure.

"A light went off then and people thought that if interest rates weren't going to be stable, you would have to be careful of bonds," Crum said. "We thought there might be a way to turn that volatility from a negative into a positive and actively manage bond portfolios."

Crum had written his graduate thesis at The University of Texas on computerized bond swapping, almost by accident. He asked a professor at UT what subject matter he could help him with in order to graduate. "I was interested in investments and people were starting to write articles on active bond management," Crum recalls. "There was a professor at Dartmouth who had written

Michael Milken proved to be a larger-than-life figure for AIM.

this rudimentary program on computerized bond swapping, and I was asked to do some simulation based on that program. I just kind of stumbled into the bond area because it was there."

After graduation, Crum started his financial career as an analyst at American General. "One day, a fellow who was managing a bond portfolio there asked me to talk to a guy who kept calling him from Drexel Burnham." It turned out to be Milken. "Six months later, the bond manager quit and the portfolio fell into my lap."

Shortly thereafter, Crum met Milken in New York and was given a copy of the book on which Milken had based his graduate thesis. "It was a study done by the National Bureau of Economic Research in terms of looking at the default rates on bonds," Crum said. "Mike is probably the smartest guy I've ever met, and I thought his ideas made sense, being able to buy undervalued bonds, bonds that other people didn't want. And the risk associated with these bonds was actually far less than the market perceived. Mike was starting to build his operation and he asked me early on if I would like to come to New York and work with him to help build a high-yield bond department, but I just had no interest."

Milken had worked as a bond sales representative for Drexel Burnham, what was then a medium-sized Philadelphia brokerage firm before it became known as Drexel Burnham Lambert. Milken was a native Californian, a graduate of Berkeley and Wharton who started working part-time in the back office at Drexel in 1969 developing a low-cost security delivery system. Shortly thereafter, he started to bring management's attention to non-investment grade securities, many of which sold at large discounts. In a 1992 interview with *Forbes*, Milken explained why junk bonds were the answers to a money manager's prayers in the late 1970s and early 1980s.

"Investors had several years' experience that had taught them that corporate bonds were a sound investment even if they weren't top-rated credits," Milken said. "In 1970 and 1974, hundreds of companies that everyone on Wall Street believed would go bankrupt didn't, and people who bought their bonds did very well. In the early 1970s, while others were telling people the sky was falling, we were saying that investing in the debt of American business was the best investment, not the worst. That was pretty good advice. Drexel published a list of high-yield bonds to buy in 1970. The list was up 40 percent in just eight months. In 1974 we did another list, which did even better."

"(Junk bonds) are a debt instrument that trades more on the underlying credit risk of the company or the industry than on movements in interest rates. They have legal characteristics of debt, but if things go bad, you're generally the first creditor to take on the rights of an equity owner."

Once AIM was created, Crum and Milken continued their association. Milken would show bond offerings to Crum, and Crum would use Drexel Burnham as one of the companies he'd sell bonds to or buy from. AIM was one of Milken's two or three largest accounts when he first started in the business.

By the time AIM appeared on the scene, Milken's business was beginning to take off. Then Crum asked him a question that changed AIM's fortunes: What would Milken think of creating a mutual fund that invests in high-yield bonds? Milken was Wall Street's hot new player, and he made a couple of trips to Houston to discuss the concept. As the weeks went by, there were phone calls back and forth and urgent messages relayed through Milken's assistant David Brown, the coverage man on the AIM account.

While the negotiations dragged on, Bauer and Graham flew to London on the Fourth of July weekend to meet with Mandy Moross and their other British stockholders. "They had made the line of credit available to us," said Graham, "but it was intended to be used for acquisitions, not to fund losses. We were rapidly depleting the amount of capital that was put in to operate the company. We needed to draw on the line of credit, and they agreed to let us put some of it against the expenses of the fund. They could just as easily have said, 'No more money. This is it.' And we would have had to close up shop rather quickly."

Back in the States, Milken paid one last visit to Houston, where Crum leveled with him: "Mike, we either have to do it now or not at all, because there won't be an AIM if we wait much longer." Milken went back to New York without committing himself. A few days later, David Brown relayed Milken's answer: "Yeah, let's do it."

Crum and Bauer traveled to New York to put together the underwriting group for the new fund before hitting the road. "On the underwriting presentations, Ted would do the introduction of who AIM is and I did all the presentations on what the products were and why we were qualified to manage it," Crum said. "When we went on the road to promote the product, we split into teams, and I focused on Texas, Florida, California, and Arizona – the retirement states – because it was a fixed-income product and we thought it would sell better in those states.

"I was teamed with a guy from Shearson named Bob Jerome. I remember doing these presentations to the point where people would applaud after it was over, and I thought, 'Well, at least we're making our points and presenting it well.' Pretty soon, Bob got all fired up about the product. I made him a bet that I would take him and his wife to dinner at 21, a famous restaurant in New York, if we raised a certain amount in the underwriting. We had raised only about $50 million with one day to go and then that last day put us over the top. I ended up having to pay off the bet."

AIM originally figured to break even if the company raised about $60 million. But the offering raised $78 million, much of which came in on the last day – September 29, 1977. "And we didn't come close to breaking even," Bauer recalled. "Still, it put blood in our veins."

High Yield Securities was an early high-water mark for AIM.

One of the reasons the fund raised more money than AIM had anticipated was because of a sales contest E.F. Hutton was conducting that ended on the day of the fund's underwriting. The contest, called "Rome or Rio," was a sales incentive program commonly used by large brokerage firms to encourage broker production. The timing of the contest couldn't have been better for AIM because it added a significant amount to AIM's initial underwriting coffers.

"We had wonderful fun when we brought High Yield Securities public," Bauer says. "We had a party the day we closed in the Board Room of the Banker's Trust Building in New York. We celebrated because if we hadn't brought that fund, we would have been out of business. We might have stayed open for another quarter, but I doubt it."

The fund's prospectus listed seven key features of High Yield Securities: high yield, diversification, economics of size, professional management, monthly income, liquidity, and special programs. Drexel Burnham was the natural choice to serve as lead underwriter for High Yield Securities, Inc., but the offering had to be cleared through the Securities and Exchange Commission. In late September, *The New York Times* called AIM legal counsel Carl Frischling about the fund, but Frischling couldn't comment because the fund was still in registration. "As a result, they slammed us," Bauer recalled. "That's when American International Group saw the similarities in our names and threatened to file suit."

Worse yet, less than 24 hours before the offering was to begin in September, Frischling received a call saying the SEC had refused to approve the deal because of what was perceived to be a little-known technicality.

"I had just talked on a nationwide telephone hookup at Shearson and was about to talk to 300 brokers in Chicago the same afternoon when Carl called up and said, 'They're not going to let you go public,'" Bauer recalled. "I went ahead and talked to the brokers, as scheduled, and many came up to me afterward and said it was the best presentation they'd ever heard. It was enough to get one's attention."

Late the same night, Frischling called Bauer to say the SEC had, indeed, changed its mind. AIM could proceed with the offering of High Yield Securities. Crum had just left a cocktail party at Drexel and was walking past the General Motors Building on Fifth Avenue in New York when the reality of the situation hit home. He was exuberant because AIM had been able to buy time with a deal that would make headlines in *The New York Times* as the first underwritten high-yield bond fund and the largest cash offering of a mutual fund in four years.

The underwriting may not have been enough to put AIM in the black, but at least the company was losing money at a slower rate. Milken also introduced AIM to potential clients, including the World Bank and Delta Airlines. Early in 1978, Drexel again underwrote a new fund for AIM, Convertible Yield Securities. This time, they managed to raise only $23 million, net of expenses.

"The concept worked well originally, but it was a very difficult one to explain to the retail customer," Graham recalls. "The fund is still in existence in a different form. We changed it to a straight convertible fund. Then we changed it to what is now known as AIM Balanced Fund, so it has grown nicely."

But it was High Yield Securities that served as AIM's first important milestone. And it also presented the company with new challenges. Along with the opportunity to place significant amounts of money under management, the fund's launch also prompted the need to print hundreds of thousands of prospectuses. Substantial costs also were incurred involving road shows – the nationwide presentations to financial advisors on the new product.

At long last, AIM had entered the world of mutual funds. And the company would never be the same.

Chapter Three

LOW FEES,
HIGH YIELDS

Despite the launch of High Yield Securities and Convertible Yield Securities in the late 1970s, it was becoming clearer that AIM could not stay on its present course and succeed. The company had not been profitable since its inception.

A typical example of AIM's folly in attempting to buy mutual funds in its early years occurred in 1979, when senior management tried to buy a closed-end fund from a California bank. "Ted and I went out there to make a presentation and we thought we'd bought it, based upon the comments of the directors since they wanted out of the business," Crum recalled.

"We had made it very clear how we were uniquely qualified to run the fund because we had run several other closed-end funds in our prior life. But when we got home, we found out it was an inside deal where the chairman of the bank eventually sold it to his son. We probably never had a chance."

Having a one-fund shop made it difficult for AIM to hire an experienced sales force. AIM's first wholesaler was Kirk Kirkpatrick, a Vietnam vet and former Air Force flight instructor. Kirkpatrick had his own dual engine plane that he used to travel to offices and make presentations. "He was quite a character who lived in Florida near Tampa," Crum said. "I was flying with him from a presentation one day and the next thing I know, we're doing a roll. It all happened so fast, but it was fun and he was a good guy. We just didn't have enough funds to make it work for him."

Indeed, AIM's early days were the emotional equivalent of a bumpy plane ride. And senior management quickly learned how to savor milestone achievements and maximize their momentum. One of the company's early victories was generated by the introduction of Short-Term Investments Company (STIC), a low-fee money market fund that undercut the competition on price. Because its costs were lower, it generated higher yields for investors. Money flowed rapidly into the fund, which was the first of AIM's institutional funds. Through the years, Fund Management Company, the institutional division of the company, would grow to be an important factor in AIM's success.

The idea for STIC arose in a conversation between Bauer and his good friend Bill Montgomery in the trust department at First City National Bank in Houston. Montgomery was the same friend who was instrumental in the acquisition of AIM's original boardroom table. He had been with Republic Bank in Dallas and had numerous friends in the trust business. Montgomery eventually joined AIM for a short time as the company's first institutional salesman and had the company's first computer.

Bill Montgomery was instrumental in AIM's early success with Short-Term Investments Company.

First City and others like it were interested in offering their trust clients the yields that were available in the money market, but they rebelled at the fees that the available money market funds were bearing. "Bill told us that he didn't like paying companies 45 basis points because all they did with the money was entertain, and he didn't need to be entertained," Bauer said.

AIM's goal was to present a plan to banks that would be extremely cost effective, one they couldn't afford to turn down. "Back then, most of the banks had a group of clerks sitting around buying commercial paper," Crum recalls. "They weren't negotiating rates or doing a good job at all. It was a cost center for the banks because they would require two or three employees to run it, and all the overhead cost money. We were able to turn it from a cost center to a profit center because they could subcontract the management of the fund to us for a relatively small amount of money."

Armed with a list of contacts in some of the larger regional banks which Montgomery had provided, Bauer went on the road and convinced five of them to participate as investors in this new money market fund. The low fee on the fund, which had breakpoints of 20, 10, and 5 basis points, raised the yield to one of the highest in the industry without having to bear any of the risks the other funds were taking to achieve higher yields. The fee schedule was unique to the industry, another tribute to Bauer's fascination with innovation.

"I remember going to one of the mutual fund conferences, and someone showed a slide of our fee schedule from the STIC prospectus and said, 'Here's a fee schedule to warm the heart of the SEC,'" Graham recalled. "I tried to slink lower in my seat because I'm sure we weren't very popular with everybody else at the time."

Carl Frischling, AIM's chief legal counsel, recalls that fund originally was met with great skepticism. "A lot of people said it was never going work because they didn't see how you could make money charging only seven or eight basis points. But I told people that all it involved was moving the decimal place over. And if the zeros are enough at the end, you're going to make money."

Bauer was talking to a prospective client who assured Bauer that his bank liked the idea, but would prefer the fund have a generic name so none of the bank's clientele would wonder who or what AIM was. That's why the original name of the fund was changed from AIM First Fiduciary Trust to Short-Term Investments Company.

"Scott Cramer, who was the head of the trust department at Wachovia, wanted to make the name of the fund innocuous and include the words 'short term' because people were familiar with short-term investments," recalls Abbott Sprague, president of Fund Management Company, AIM's institutional subsidiary. "I think that really made us unique within most of the institutional business in that our fund's name is generic."

AIM's five original clients were First City National Bank of Houston, Trust Company Bank of Georgia, Wachovia National, Liberty Bank in Oklahoma, and the First National Bank of Dallas. Quickly thereafter, Valley National Bank in Arizona climbed aboard. At the time, money was flowing out of many money market funds, especially those sponsored by brokerage firms into direct investments in the stock and bond markets. Such funds' yields were suffering because they had no new money to invest in the rising interest rate environment that prevailed. STIC, on the other hand, was the beneficiary of large inflows of money and was able to continually buy portfolio instruments at the higher rates, thereby augmenting its already high yield.

"It's sometimes better to be lucky than good," Sprague said. "We were lucky that we were getting money in during a period of rising interest rates versus getting money in during a period of declining interest rates. In the latter case, funds underperform as new assets come in."

Just before the fund was to be launched, news broke that Institutional Liquid Assets, a fund run by Salomon Brothers for the First National Bank of Chicago, had become the first institutional fund to break its $1.00 net asset value by going too far out on the yield curve. Bauer knew the timing of that news had the potential to kill STIC before the fund was even launched, and decided to add a new, unique twist to the fund. Bauer called all of the institutions with whom AIM had a verbal handshake and told them the fund wouldn't have an average maturity of

Ted Bauer directed AIM's early strategy sessions in the 1970s.
Left to right, Gary Crum, Bob Graham, Bauer, fixed-income analyst
Steve Pouns, and money market trader Chris Jessee.
Pouns and Jessee were two of AIM's early employees.

more than 40 days. Moreover, the fund's portfolio would not have any securities with a maturity of more than 60 days. That move assuaged potential fears and helped provide AIM a much-needed niche in the marketplace.

The AIM team that managed the money market fund was a professional one that created a research staff which performed its own independent write-ups and credit work on all securities considered for the fund's portfolio. The SEC later required all companies to follow a similar process. The team followed Bauer's philosophy that the "best is none too good for money market funds."

AIM launched STIC on November 4, 1980, the day Ronald Reagan was elected to his first term as president. "Wachovia called one day and said, 'We'll be giving you $5 million a day,'" Graham recalls. "And somebody asked,

'For how many days?' Their response was, 'For a long time!' And the money just kept coming in and coming in, until it built up to several hundred million."

December marked AIM's first monthly profit since the company's inception as $325 million came in the first month. At the beginning of 1981, AIM owed a total of $175,000 in current debt. By the end of March, it had been paid in full.

"The fund grew so fast that we all were astounded," recalls Steve Turman, one of STIC's research analysts. "It was mainly due to the efforts of Bill Montgomery, who was a true statesman, a gentleman from the word go. When he ran the trust department at First City Bank, so much money poured in from them in six months, the research barely mattered. He was a big, gray-haired man with a baritone bull voice who knew everybody in the trust business in Texas. Of course, this was before so many Texas banks went belly up.

"When Bill Montgomery was out there, the money came to us in droves. He just commanded a room the way Ted Bauer does. When he came to work for us, I never heard him say an unkind word about anyone, anywhere, and he had ample chances to do so. Other companies knew they were dealing with somebody who was shooting straight all the time.

"I remember one story when I went to Amarillo to meet Bill. I only had about four customers there from when I was selling bonds. I was a young guy, probably wearing a polyester suit with a polyester tie. Bill was really just putting up with me because I truly had a diction problem. Bill flew his own plane, a twin-engine Piper or Cessna, but on the way back he let me take the controls.

*With Bill Montgomery at the controls, AIM reached new
heights in institutional sales in the 1980s.*

"I ended up taking lessons, and I was three hours away
from getting my license when I decided to quit. I wasn't
worried about myself, but I was afraid of killing someone
on the ground. But Bill got me interested in flying. He
gave me a crystal clock in the shape of a plane. It doesn't
work anymore, but I keep it in the office because it
reminds me of him."

Thanks in part to Montgomery's efforts, the success of
STIC had unintended beneficial side effects for AIM. It
gave Bauer the opportunity to get on the road and give
the company more exposure and it also gave brokers
more of a reason to call on an up-and-coming money
market manager. Relationships were developed with
Salomon Brothers, Goldman Sachs, and First Boston.
Major firms that historically hadn't called AIM now had
reason to do so. The assets of AIM's money market funds
implied the company was a major player when, in reality,
revenues were still quite low.

AIM's next foray into money market funds resulted from Bauer's longtime friendship with Bart Harvey, who was managing partner of Alex. Brown. Bauer had met Harvey in Baltimore in the 1950s and they used to travel together once a year as part of an investment club. "I had been needling him for a long time about managing a money market fund for Alex. Brown," Bauer says. "We went to Nassau with the club in the spring of 1981, and he turned to me at lunch one day and said, 'I want you to have our money market fund.'" The Alex. Brown Cash Reserve Fund started on September 1, 1981, took in $500 million by year-end, and one time reached a peak of $2 billion in assets. AIM ran the fund for 11 years.

In 1984, AIM joined Provident Mutual Life Insurance Company of Philadelphia to create Cortland Financial Group, Inc. AIM assisted Cortland Financial Group in the creation of a three money market series of funds – prime, government, and tax-free – designed for use by broker/dealer firms for the cash balances of their customers. The funds ultimately grew to more than $1 billion in assets. Two years later, AIM established the Silver Star Fund, a private label money-market fund for the First Republic Bank of Dallas. First Republic then became part of NCNB, which then became NationsBank and, ultimately, Bank of America. AIM served as administrator and distributor for the Silver Star Fund, which later became the Hatteras Fund and, at one time, had almost to $2 billion in assets.

Bauer even appeared in local television commercials promoting money-market funds in the early '80s. AIM's money-market assets under management subsequently increased to almost $15 billion. But the assets grew to the

*Carl Frischling has provided AIM with sage legal
advice for almost a quarter century.*

point that AIM became victimized by its own success.
"Alex. Brown and NationsBank took them in-house after
they realized they could make more money running the
funds themselves," Crum recalls.

By the early 1990s, AIM no longer served as administrator for the Cortland Financial Group or the NationsBank
funds and also had stopped managing the Alex. Brown
Cash Reserve Fund. "There wasn't much revenue there,
but the assets made us look big on the Street, and that
was important," Bauer says. Over the years, AIM has
remained a prominent figure in the management of institutional money market funds. The company had more
than $50 billion in money market assets under manage-
ment by the middle of 2000.

Chapter Four

CHAIRMAN OF
THE BOARD

Before there was a concept called the Global Economy, almost before a company called AIM Management Group had left the runway, there was a trail that led from South Africa to England to New York to Houston.

As a New World commuter, Mandy Moross wanted to own 75 percent of AIM's stock, a compliment to the idea and those who nurtured it. Ted Bauer told him, "No, this has to be an American company. The management and other Houston backers have to represent the majority of ownership."

What they didn't want was a cult of personality, big thunder echoing down from the rafters of the penthouse floor. Bob Graham and Gary Crum inspire confidence and admiration. Bauer inspires devotion. But there is no cult at AIM. There isn't even a penthouse.

Ted Bauer was well-connected, and now he truly needed to be. Which is where Manfred (Mandy) Moross came into the picture. A man of modest height, with a solid build, Moross is the kind of fellow who can charm a pocket-handkerchief out of a silkworm. He was one of the youngest students, at 20, and the first South African, ever accepted by Harvard Business School.

As a boy, he worked in the gold mines – in the office – although it would not be a stretch to picture Mandy with goggles and a pick. He made his first wealth in South Africa, in insurance and banking, then sold it all, moved to Britain and did it again. He is the kind of man, who, to give his three sons and daughter a worldly education, sent one son to The University of Texas and his daughter to Rice.

Moross had started what the British called a unit trust business – what Americans refer to as mutual funds. He looked across the Atlantic and set his sights on America, and this was the real genesis of AIM. He was about to cross paths with Ted Bauer.

"One of the bankers I used," Moross recalled from his New York offices, "was Lehman Brothers. There was a chap called George Heiman, who was the new senior partner there. The chairman was Pete Peterson, who had been Secretary of the Treasury in the Eisenhower cabinet.

"They brought to my attention the possibility of acquiring the mutual fund activity from the American General Insurance Group in Houston. And Ted, at that time, was the head of it…and also ready to leave."

Mandy soon realized that he and American General were oceans apart, and no deal could be done. Soon after, at the urging of intermediaries, Bauer flew to New York to meet this traveled, cultured South African. They hit it off instantly. "Before he left," said Mandy Moross, "Ted said,

*Mandy Moross, a true business globetrotter,
gave AIM a worldly view as chairman of the board.*

'Look, if we decide to go it alone, would you back us?'
And I said, 'Yes.'

"Bauer was a man of considerable quality, which meant
more to me than education, history or background.
When you have been in major businesses all over the
world, you learn that the most important ingredient is
always the man. If you team up with the right people, you
have a ball. If not, you have anxiety and aggravation.

"Many people think Ted Bauer is a great, outgoing,
expansive guy. Actually, he is very reserved, a humble
man of great character and integrity. He's all of that. So
we decided to put the business together.

"All of the guys, Ted, Bob, Gary, or Steve Pouns, who
was part of the original group, took modest salaries and
stayed with them. Also, which was important to me, they
paid for their interest in the business. Not all of them had
the money to do it. So they had to beg or borrow, what-

ever they had to do, to find the money to invest. They were all quality guys and they were a good team.

"I had brought in a partner or two, and there was a Houston investor, and they dropped out along the way. I stayed in. For the first five years we had losses, and I funded the losses. I believed in them and the kind of people they were. I knew it was just a question of time. America was the most equity-minded nation in the world."

Partnerships can be difficult, and worse. If Sean Penn and Madonna couldn't make it, what chance do ordinary people have? But instantly, Ted Bauer and Mandy Moross recognized a kindred spirit. Ted was tall and gangly, with a quick wit. Mandy had the build and bounce of a good middleweight boxer, and a gentle nature. Both dressed like members of Parliament.

"He's a great man," says Bauer, whose judgments tend to be kind, but not thoughtless. "He's very intelligent. We just clicked. I went to Harvard. He went to Harvard Business. Both of us could handle ourselves. We had the same goals, and we needed each other to reach them. One thing I knew was that you had to start with a big financial background. We had that."

If one believed in omens, the deal might never have happened. On his first visit to Houston, Moross took suddenly ill. "He fainted," recalled Bauer. "I picked him up, literally, and carried him in my arms to the car and took him to Twelve Oaks Hospital. Later, they found out he had an inner-ear problem."

But Bauer was quickly reassured that Mandy's hearing had been undamaged. "When he agreed to back us, I asked him if he knew what he was doing. He said, 'Yes.' I said, 'Fine, you're going to be taking a big risk.'"

*French Peterson, left, and Manfred Gorvy. They joined
Mandy Moross among a small group of original investors in AIM.*

There were times, Bauer sensed, when Mandy grew
weary of "the losses, the struggling." But he persevered
through all of it, the ups and downs, the in-betweens. He
had two qualities you always look for in a backer – wealth
and staying power. He could afford to feel weary or impatient. He could afford to feel bored or even sleepy. The
key was, he never felt indifferent, always supportive.

"When we bought him out in 1993, he did it to
accommodate the other key people in the company, who
had earned the right to have a fairer share of the rewards.
It was a generous thing to do."

There was no ceremony the day Mandy stepped
down as chairman, nor did he want one. Nevertheless, his
partners presented him with a gift: a large, engraved, silver
and crystal block from Tiffany's.

A class gift for a class individual.

Chapter Five

FROM BOOM
TO BUST

Houston's economy was the envy of the nation in 1979. The price of oil had skyrocketed, eventually reaching $38 per barrel, and AIM had trouble keeping secretaries because they kept getting better offers from oil companies that didn't care what they paid. Companies kept expanding, pushing the price of real estate upward. AIM began to feel the squeeze in its 16-person Dresser Tower office in downtown Houston when the company was told there was no space for further growth.

"We went over and looked at Allen Center, a property owned by Ken Schnitzer, but it was more than we wanted to pay," Crum said. "A couple of days later, a real estate broker called and told us Schnitzer also owned Greenway Plaza, which was more in the price range of what we were looking for. A new building had been finished next to the Coastal Tower only a block from The Summit, where the Houston Rockets played.

"Our first reaction was, 'Why would anybody want to be on the Southwest Freeway?' We were concerned about having to move because so many people were coming into Houston at the time and the freeways were becoming more and more congested. There was a recession in the Rust Belt. People were leaving the Midwest, putting everything they had in a U-HAUL, and coming down here to work in the oil industry."

Bauer and Crum each drove past Greenway Plaza during rush hour a couple of times to see if the bumper-to-bumper nightmares they'd heard were true. But they weren't, and AIM prepared to move its headquarters and prepare for expansion. "We thought if we could cut down on the commute time on the freeways, it would serve everybody best," Crum said. "The decision to move to Greenway Plaza has served us well over the years."

The company moved into the Summit Tower at 11 Greenway Plaza on May 30, 1980. AIM took space on the vacant 19th floor, which meant longer elevator rides for AIM's modest-but-growing workforce that had been located on the 10th floor of Dresser Tower. "I was a little concerned about being as high as the 19th floor because fire ladders only go up so far," recalls Judy Creel, AIM's director of corporate resources. "But we found out that twin towers were going to be built about 12 stories tall that would block our view, and we wanted to see over them."

AIM chose the northeast corner of the floor, which provided a view of downtown Houston, and 1976 as its suite number to represent the year AIM was founded. But that caused a problem for building management, which said AIM couldn't use an even number for its primary mailing address if the company's offices were on that side of the floor – it had to come up with an odd number. The solution? The suite number was changed to 1919 because it was Bauer's birth year.

Once he moved into his office, Bauer had a panoramic view of Houston's rapid growth. Building cranes dotted the landscape in every direction as a result of surging oil prices. The resulting demand for labor was so great that two entrepreneurs from Michigan came up with a remarkable idea that perhaps best illustrated the contrast between Houston's robust economic health and the recession that had hit a majority of the country.

Every Thursday, two truckers would leave Michigan in an 18-wheeler and arrive in Houston early Saturday morning in time to purchase the early Sunday edition of the *Houston Chronicle*, which had one of the largest classified ad sections of any newspaper in the country. The sections were printed in the wee hours of Saturday morning, filled with help-wanted ads that wouldn't receive much attention in an already tight job market. At the time, the Sunday papers in Houston cost only 50 cents.

The truckers would buy thousands of copies of the paper at face value at the *Chronicle* loading dock Saturday and drive back to Michigan as fast as they could. They'd arrive at an advertised location in suburban Detroit on Sunday and meet throngs of job-seekers willing to pay $3 each for a classified ad section they could scan and make phone calls about prospective jobs in Houston first thing Monday morning. The situation repeated itself week after week for many months, earning the truckers a six-figure income.

Although AIM was growing at a much slower pace than the oil companies that composed a large part of Houston's economy, it needed the extra space Greenway Plaza had to offer because it had just won the Delta

Judy Creel, AIM's director of corporate resources, had a bird's-eye view of Houston's growth in the early 1980s.

Airlines and World Bank high-yield accounts. "We had decided to go with the presumption that we were going to survive," Crum says. "But we also made a selfish determination that it was better to have an office close to where the principals of the company lived. When we first went downtown in 1976, we felt we had to make a statement. But in reality, it didn't matter those first few years because we had few visitors."

One of the reasons AIM had received little attention in its early years was because the company had experienced a notable lack of success in acquiring any equity funds. On several occasions, fund groups withdrew from negotiations at the last minute with AIM in order to give it one more try on their own. Other times, acquisitions were made directly with major firms and AIM had no opportunity to bid.

A sign of the times: AIM's move to 11 Greenway Plaza was reflective of the company's plans to expand into retail mutual funds.

But in November 1979, after failing to buy six other equity funds, AIM purchased the Edson Gould Fund. It was a small-company growth fund, created and managed by the venerable Edson Gould, who had predicted the Crash of '29 and the traumatic bear market of 1973-74. AIM paid $50,000 for the fund, which had $5 million in assets. At the time, AIM had no sales reps and no wholesalers. "The sales force was essentially Gary and me begging and pleading," Bauer said.

Gould was in his 70s when AIM bought the fund that bore his name from a company called Anametrics. But Gould was seldom seen by AIM personnel before, during, or after the transaction. Gould's business manager, Steven Greenberg, had an office in New York that had once been used by fight promoter Don King.

Gould had earned legendary status on Wall Street as a technical analyst because of his uncanny success as a market sage. He used to predict market reversals based on various decisions of the Federal Reserve. According to Gould, if the Federal Reserve raised the discount rate three times, it was indicative of a tightening of the money supply, leading to a bear market. If the Federal Reserve cut the discount rate three times, it indicated a loosening of the money market, leading to a bull market.

In 1979, the year AIM bought the Edson Gould Fund, Gould forecast a rise in the Dow Jones Industrial Average from the then 800 area to above 3700 in the 1990s. The prediction was regarded by many investors and analysts as a "mad bull's pipe dream." But Gould's prediction eventually came true when the Dow hit 3700 on November 16, 1993.

Unfortunately for AIM, the Edson Gould Fund didn't make as much noise. "It did well for a while and then it went dead," Bauer said. "On top of that, we ran into a bad market and the fund had all sorts of SEC problems that had been dumped on us. We decided to change the name of the fund to the Greenway Fund, but that didn't have much of an effect." The fund eventually was sold years later to Provident Mutual for $200,000.

Nevertheless, the message was clear: AIM had begun to move into the equity aspect of asset management in addition to managing high-yield bonds and money market funds. "We weren't going to disappear," recalls Abbott Sprague. "It wasn't long before a lot of people who had laughed at us and said, 'Call me when you get some *real* money' began to pay attention to us."

An ongoing need to diversify its source of revenue prompted AIM to introduce AIM Summit Fund in 1982. The fund was an equity fund sold as a contractual plan product uniquely suited to systematic purchases by U.S. military personnel. The fund was named after the arena in

Greenway Plaza which served as home to the Houston Rockets of the NBA. Increased revenue from load funds, private accounts, and other assets was necessary for AIM in order to balance fees from money market funds.

"We were managing money market funds for InterFirst Bank in Fort Worth, which had a relationship with USPA (United Services Planning Association, Inc.), Crum said. "Officials from USPA wanted to know if InterFirst could run a mutual fund product for them that would be sold to personnel in the U.S. Armed Forces, but banks weren't allowed to run mutual funds in those days. That's when InterFirst came to us and asked us if we could be partners."

AIM liked the idea for several reasons. First, it would enable the company to broaden its product line. Second, the very nature of a contractual plan appeared to be a win-win situation for AIM and fund shareholders. Shareholders would dollar-cost-average into the fund in the form of monthly contributions of at least $50 for a 15-year period from Individual Retirement Accounts (IRAs).

It was hoped that AIM Summit Fund would grow to $50 million in assets within four years, but much of the commission after costs would have to be reserved against potential cancellation of individual plans purchased in their early stage. In actuality, the fund reached $72 million in four years and crossed the $2.5 billion mark in 1999, despite the fact contractual plans were not available in all 50 states. When contractual plans became available in California for the first time in more than 50 years, a consultant stayed up on New Year's Eve in 1994 so he could sell a Summit Investors Plan just after midnight when the law took effect.

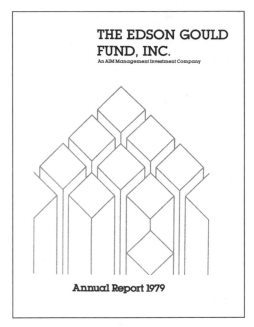

THE EDSON GOULD FUND, INC.
An AIM Management Investment Company

Annual Report 1979

The Edson Gould Fund was AIM's first equity fund.

David Barnard, a Vietnam War veteran, assumed responsibilities as lead portfolio manager for AIM Summit Fund in 1995. While serving as an infantryman in Vietnam in the 1960s, Barnard had read a book that had arrived free in the mailbag. *Reminiscences of a Stock Operator* was a fictionalized biography of master speculator Jesse Livermore and remains one of the most widely read and recommended investment books of all time. After reading the book, Barnard became fascinated by the possibility of creating wealth through stock investing.

The book recounts Livermore's mastery of the markets beginning when he was just 14 years old. In a lifetime spent on Wall Street, Livermore made and lost four stock market fortunes. In 1906, he made $250,000 by going short on Union Pacific just before the San Francisco earthquake. In 1925, he made $10 million trading grain. In 1929, he lost the lot and was widely blamed for the crash that triggered the Great Depression. At particularly low ebb in 1940, he said good-bye to his third wife, checked into a Manhattan hotel, and shot himself.

When he left the Army, Barnard visited a PaineWebber broker in Muskegon, Michigan, to ask his advice about getting into the money management business. The broker advised Barnard to get an education. So he did, studying finance, accounting, and economics, completing both an undergraduate degree and an MBA at Western Michigan.

After graduation, Barnard worked for small financial companies, including a bank and an investment management firm, where he was able to gain a great deal of varied experience in a short time. He was managing convertible portfolios for a bank in Huntington, Ohio, when Gary Crum called to see if he'd be interested in joining AIM.

"David was recommended to us by John Freund, who covered us for Salomon Brothers," Crum recalled. "Jack Painter had run our convertible funds from the get-go in 1978, but Jack had decided to leave us to run convert portfolios in Atlanta. Jack ended up trading options on the Chicago Board."

Barnard was one of the first portfolio managers assigned to work with Harry Hutzler on the Weingarten Fund in the mid-1980s and also served as co-manager of AIM Constellation Fund for almost 10 years. A major proponent of technology, Barnard was named lead portfolio manager for AIM Global Telecommunications and Technology Fund in 1999.

While AIM's offices were frequently reconfigured to accommodate new employees for the growing company in the mid-'80s, Houston's oil boom had gone bust. Oil prices had plunged to $14 a barrel and stayed well below their all-time highs for the better part of two decades. In fact, when Creel celebrated her 20th anniversary as an AIM employee in 1999, oil prices were still lower than when she first walked through AIM's doors. Real estate values went into a ditch, and entire office buildings were empty, with months of free space being offered as an inducement to prospective tenants. The city's employment situation had gone from one end of the spectrum to the other in only a few short years.

"I'll tell you something sad," Bauer said. "When Houston was blowing up, we put an ad in the paper for an accountant. We had 125 responses. It was sad for the city, but very lucky for AIM. Houston had the finest labor pool in the land. We were fortunate to be able to grow during a period when there was no direct competition."

The local economic situation was perhaps best captured by a joke that had two well-to-do matrons shopping in downtown Houston, when a frog hopped between them. "I'm not really a frog," he pleaded. "I'm actually a wealthy Texas oilman. A witch put a spell on me. If one of you will kiss me, I'll turn back into an oilman."

Without breaking stride, one of the ladies picked up the frog, opened the clasp on her purse, plopped him in, and snapped the purse shut. With a quizzical look, her friend asked, "Aren't you going to kiss him?"

"Heck, no!" the woman replied. "Right now, a talking frog is worth a lot more than a Texas oilman!"

Chapter Six

LIGHTNING IN
A BOTTLE

As its reputation surged, AIM began to build a stable of mutual funds around low-cost, fixed-income and money-market funds, mostly geared toward institutional investors. By the end of 1985, the company had expanded to 60 employees, and assets had climbed to $6.4 billion. Company debt had been reduced to $1.5 million, and AIM had been able to pay its first dividends to shareholders in 1984 and 1985.

But in the mutual fund game, AIM was still relatively small. And senior management knew a different door would soon have to open if the company was to continue to grow. It simply couldn't rely solely on its institutional and separate accounts. For AIM to be a long-term survivor in the money management business, the time had come for the company to make a splash in the retail marketplace.

Although AIM's founders had coveted retail funds for years, they hadn't been very successful in acquiring retail products. By mid-1985, however, a sense of urgency had

Gary Crum, left, and Chris Jessee. Crum kept helping search for ways AIM could earn the corporate stability it needed in the mid-1980s.

taken root. There were signs that some of the relationships AIM had built in the institutional and separate account business were becoming increasingly unstable. Crum, for one, had learned first-hand how money could flow out as fast as it came in, and often on short notice.

"I remember sitting around and thinking, 'Where are we going to go with this business?'" Crum said. "We had two old retail funds in Convertible Yield Securities and High Yield Securities that had basically gone nowhere. And we also had separate accounts. But we'd already been through enough trauma with the separate account business to know that you could be fired for doing too good a job, and that just didn't seem right."

Harry Hutzler, left, and Julian Lerner provided AIM with the portfolio management experience it needed to make a bold entry into equity markets.

The definitive example of how AIM could be victimized by its own success in the separate account business came the day Crum received a call from Hilda Ochoa of World Bank. Michael Milken originally had recommended AIM to World Bank in 1979, and World Bank subsequently had placed $5 million with AIM to manage in a hybrid account of convertible and high-yield securities. Securing such a prestigious account was one of the reasons AIM was able to move from downtown Houston to Greenway Plaza in 1980. The World Bank account grew more than tenfold over the next few years and was regarded as one of AIM's crown jewels. But World Bank's business also was regarded as difficult to retain, which left more than $50 million in assets vulnerable.

"One day, Hilda called me up and said, 'Gary, you've had a great year, but we're taking your account away,'" Crum recalled. "I said, 'Hilda, that doesn't make any sense. Most of the time you do something well, you're rewarded with even more.' But she said World Bank had decided to change its asset allocation. She said AIM had done so well, that World Bank didn't think we could continue to perform at that level. I asked Hilda if they could just leave in the amount they originally gave us. They agreed to do that for about a year, then took it all away.

"That whole situation was a real eye-opener. I felt the whole system was backward. You never really knew what was going on behind the scenes. People a lot larger than us were out there entertaining people on 100-foot yachts trying to get and keep separate account business. It was obvious that you had to be able to play that game well if you were going to play it at all. I kept asking myself, 'Do we want to put up with all of those irrational decisions?'"

AIM's intent to diversify its business and bolster its presence in the retail marketplace led to an interesting turn of events that would shape the company's destiny for the remainder of the millennium. On an autumn day in 1985, Bauer placed a call to AIM legal counsel Carl Frischling, who was closely associated with the Lexington Funds. Frischling had been with the Channing Funds when American General Insurance Company acquired the funds and Bauer was made interim president of Channing Management in 1969.

Bauer called Frischling to learn if the Lexington Funds would soon be for sale. Although Frischling said he didn't think so, he said he had just received a call from somebody who might be interested in selling the Weingarten Equity Fund and the Constellation Growth Fund.

"There was this lawyer friend of mine who used to represent a company called Weingarten Management and he said they needed a little ERISA help," Frischling recalls. "He said the company representing them at the time didn't have any ERISA (Employee Retirement Income Security

Act) expertise. So I called them, gave them some advice, and thought that was the end of it." The next day, Lew Sonn, the business manager for Weingarten Management, called Frischling with a different question. Sonn said he was dealing with an SEC-related matter and needed a second opinion from Frischling.

"He told me about these two funds that he and his partner were interested in selling because the going prices at the time were rather high and neither of them had any heirs. Later that day, Ted called and asked about Lexington. I told him, 'Forget about Lexington. I have something that should be of interest to you.' And that's what started the Weingarten acquisition."

At the time, the Weingarten Fund owned one of the mutual fund industry's best 10-year performance records with an average annual total return of 24.6 percent. Weingarten was a large-cap fund that originally had been organized in 1967 as the Compufund. It changed its name to Weingarten in 1969, three years after portfolio manager Heinz Hutzler, better known to his friends as Harry, left Value Line and joined a small New York brokerage firm named Weingarten & Company.

Hutzler had started his career as an economist with Value Line in 1953 and was instrumental in developing that company's now-famous timeliness ranking for individual stocks. The Constellation Fund also was having a good year in 1985, and would finish with a total return of 28.4 percent, making it the top-performing aggressive growth fund for the year of funds between $50 million and $100 million in net assets. Both funds were managed out of New York.

The reason for the funds' success was directly related to Hutzler's management style. A short, round-faced

Educated as an engineer, Bob Graham complemented Ted Bauer's visionary skills by constructing ways to help AIM reach its corporate goals.

man, Hutzler had fled Germany before World War II. He was a scholar, fluent in several languages, an expert bridge player, and a collector of rare books. He also was an expert on the laws of statistical probability.

Hutzler's earnings-momentum philosophy dictated that a manager should buy stocks at the first sign of earnings improvement and sell when earnings first declined. On Wall Street, there tends to be a greater emphasis on what stocks to buy than there is on what stocks to sell. But Hutzler maintained that knowing when to sell was just as critical to the overall success of a portfolio. A decelerating trend in a company's earnings would prompt Hutzler to sell a stock. He believed that poor earnings reports would reflect fundamental problems within the company, such as a decline in its sales or profit margins.

By adhering to this system, a portfolio manager was not allowed to maintain emotional ties to any individual stock or hang on to a company that was underperforming.

Specifically, Hutzler looked for two types of stocks. He liked to buy core companies that had grown at least 16 percent per year for 10 years and were expected to grow at least that much for the next five years according to analysts' forecasts. He also liked to buy companies whose quarterly earnings come out substantially better than analysts had forecast. Hutzler called that "the surprise factor." But before buying the stock, Hutzler would check to make sure the increase came from operating earnings and not from a sale of assets. He would then hold the stock at least three months until the next earnings report, and often longer.

"Research has shown that very often, when there is one earnings surprise, it will be followed by another," Hutzler said. "The reason is that if there is a fundamental change in a company, analysts may be slow in adjusting to it." Hutzler's philosophy was the antithesis of the efficient market theory, which argues that everything known about a company is already included in the price of its shares. But academic studies had shown over the years that companies whose quarterly earnings exceeded expectations regularly do better than the market in the following six months. That's the strategy Hutzler relied on for big gains.

"My experience has been that buying stocks after an earnings surprise provides about a 60 percent success rate," Hutzler said. "That is, about 60 percent will do better than the market and about 40 percent will do worse than the market. That may not sound very impressive, but you can get very good results from a 60-percent success rate

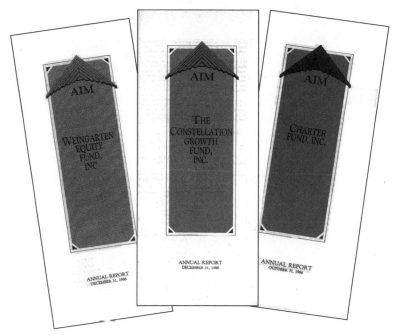

Three aces: The first shareholder reports for AIM's new Weingarten, Constellation, and Charter Funds.

if you let the profits run after you find an earnings surprise." Perhaps the greatest tribute to Hutzler's management style can be traced to Constellation's returns in 1979 and 1980, when the fund had annual total returns of 76.8 percent and 74.4 percent, respectively.

Bauer seized the moment after his phone conversation with Frischling. "With all due respect to Harry and Lew, they didn't have any infrastructure with their funds," Frischling said. "That's why they were very limited in how big they were ever going to get, and Ted knew it. As talented as he is, Ted has always known that he can't do things by himself in this business. We used to think of a mutual fund business as a three-legged stool consisting of marketing/distribution, administration, and investments."

Bauer quickly contacted Hutzler and Sonn and scheduled a lunch meeting at the Bankers Trust Building in New York. The idea of buying equity funds with proven track records and very little overhead was of tremendous appeal to a company trying to make a big splash. And Bauer was determined to buy the two funds from Hutzler, even though his idea met with early opposition.

"I was never as firmly in favor of acquiring the Weingarten and Constellation Funds as Ted was," recalled Graham, who accompanied Bauer on the trip to New York. "Ted had an expression he liked to use that young people back then had never seen a bull market. Well, now there's a saying that a lot of young people have never seen a bear market. But Ted knew what could happen with a bull market and was confident it was the right thing to do."

Within 24 hours, a deal had been reached under which AIM would purchase the Weingarten Fund and the Constellation Fund for $9 million, or approximately four times annual earnings. "That was the high end of the scale," Bauer said, "but the funds had terrific records." In addition to acquiring the funds, AIM also retained the services of Hutzler, who would remain as a portfolio manager and mentor to the younger managers AIM wanted to have follow in his footsteps. Hutzler eventually would retire in 1993.

On almost a parallel course to AIM's acquisition of Weingarten and Constellation was the company's decision to purchase the Charter Fund from Julian Lerner, whom Bauer had known since the 1970s. Lerner called Bauer in late 1985 trying to interest AIM in the Associated Planners Fund, on which Lerner had been serving as sub-advisor. "Julian called us about that other fund, but I told Bob, 'Wait and see. I'm going to buy the Charter Fund.' And within three days, we had a deal."

Bauer's interest in the fund was easy to understand. Charter had been selected to the *Forbes'* honor roll five times between 1970 and 1982, during which time the fund had produced an average annual total return of 18 percent despite the horrendous bear market of 1973-74.

Lerner was a native Texan, born in Galveston and educated as a lawyer. He learned about mutual funds from a client and started the Charter Fund in 1968 with $1,000 of his own money and about $1 million invested by a group of life insurance companies. He first wanted to name the fund the Royal Fund after University of Texas football coach Darrell Royal. He also liked the name "University Fund." After learning both names were spoken for, he leafed through the thick A.M. Best book of insurance companies, looking for ideas. He found Charter. "I thought it was a neat name," he recalled.

Lerner managed the Charter Fund out of Dallas, bought out his investors in 1975, and acted as a one-man mutual fund company for 11 years. He performed every task from fund management to administration. He decided to sell Charter to AIM only 30 minutes into his initial conversation with Bauer because he realized he alone could not provide the distribution the growing fund needed. At the time AIM bought the Charter Fund, the Fund had about 12,000 shareholders and $75 million in net assets.

"My original plan was to reach $25 million in assets and make a living," Lerner said. He based his management style on his unshakable opposition to losing money. Lerner liked large-cap stocks rather than small ones. He

Ted Bauer can have his cake and eat it, too: AIM observes its 10th anniversary and prepares to enter the equity mutual fund business in a big way in August 1986.

avoided high-tech stocks because he couldn't understand what the companies were producing. "I can't work my computer," he was once quoted as saying. "I've got one, but I don't know how to use it." Lerner eventually retired from AIM Charter Fund in 1994.

AIM paid $3 million for the Charter Fund and the Associated Planners Fund, the latter of which AIM sold to Chase Bank soon afterward. AIM immediately placed sales charges on all three funds and prepared to start marketing the funds through financial advisors. Adding all three funds to its product line at once was like catching lightning in a bottle. The Weingarten, Constellation, and Charter Funds all had superior records and no baggage in terms of excess employees.

"The key aspect of the purchase of the Weingarten, Constellation, and Charter Funds was the decision to keep the existing managers on board as a basis for being able to sell the product more favorably to the investor, and then use those people to train the managers who came after them," says Bill Kleh, who joined AIM as chief legal counsel in 1986. "A lot of groups with huge egos invested in their business would have just gone out and acquired the assets and not maintained the presence of the managers."

At long last, AIM was about to enter the highly competitive equity fund business. But that also meant the company would have to spend millions of dollars to build a sales force and develop sales literature of high interest.

AIM officially took over the Weingarten, Constellation, and Charter Funds at the end of April 1986. Within six months, the company had hired a field staff of six wholesalers, all of whom quickly learned that mutual fund investors still had a much heartier appetite for fixed-income products than equity funds. The funds eventually would grow from a combined $345 million to $42 billion in net assets by 2000, but success didn't come quickly. "For a while," recalled Jim Salners, one of AIM's original six wholesalers, "trying to sell Weingarten, Constellation, and Charter was like trying to sell ice to the Eskimos."

Chapter Seven

THE ODD
COUPLE

Part of the appeal of buying the Weingarten and Constellation Funds was the fact both funds had superb performance records. But equally as important was Harry Hutzler's decision to remain with AIM and tutor an apprentice who ultimately would take over both funds when he retired. Hutzler was in his early 60s when the two funds were sold to AIM, so the meter was running.

Shortly after AIM consummated the purchase of Weingarten and Constellation, the company began looking for someone who could organize a trading desk for its growing equity fund business. The search led to a young trader at American General in Houston. Jonathan Schoolar had graduated from The University of Texas with a degree in chemical engineering, just in time to catch the collapse of the world oil markets. He had been at American General for three years when Gary Crum called to say AIM was going to enter the equity market in a meaningful way.

"I did a lot of interviews when I graduated from UT," Schoolar reflects. "I remember someone telling me, 'Son, I have nothing for you. I am laying off people who worked for me for 30 years.' So I went back to business school in 1983 and then I was one semester into grad school when a trading job came open with American General. I remember the first time I walked onto the trading floor, and guys were yelling and screaming and throwing phones, and I thought, 'Well, I can do that! That looks like fun! And, they were going to pay me, instead of my having to pay tuition. So I dropped out of graduate school.

"I had been wanting to get out of trading and into portfolio management. I didn't know how to do it and, in all truth, I probably couldn't make that move today. But the mutual fund business was wide open. It was kind of like the oil business in Houston in the late 1960s. You know, if you had a pickup truck and $100, you were in the oil business. In mutual funds, you just jumped in and made it go.

"In the meantime, I had started to research the performance rankings. I started pulling out the names of no-load funds with good track records and made a list of maybe 25, just to get a feel for it. Then Gary called and said they were getting into the equity business and did I want to talk?"

Schoolar was curious. He asked Crum how AIM, which had been regarded as a fixed-income shop, was going to make the move into equities. Crum responded that AIM had just purchased three equity funds and retained the two portfolio managers associated with the funds – Harry Hutzler, in New York, and Julian Lerner, in Dallas. Schoolar asked Crum what funds they managed.

"And he said, 'Weingarten, Constellation, and Charter,'" Schoolar said. "The first two happened to be on my list.

"We met at an Astros game and Gary made an offer. I said, 'That's a lateral move,' and he said, 'Well, that's what it pays.' So I joined AIM in August of 1986."

The education of Jon Schoolar reinforced Ted Bauer's concept that "People are the product." "The idea was that I would put together the trading floor," Schoolar said. "But in the back of my mind, I wanted to learn how to manage money. First, I had to get over the shock of how small AIM really was. I had come from a firm that was, I think, the largest mutual fund company in the South. I was used to resources and machines.

"My first couple of weeks, I literally had to design the forms for making trades. I was thinking that I had gotten in way over my head. I didn't know what I was doing. But we got through that, mainly because the two money managers were superb, not only as stock pickers, but as people. That was probably the key to AIM's success.

"If you remember the mid-'80s, it was all power lunches, yellow ties, slick black hair, and that sort of thing. I was so tired of all that. So here were Harry and Julian in their mid-60s with the knowledge they had to start training a new group. I hit it off with Harry because I was real burned out on the whole Wall Street thing in New York. Harry was the antithesis of Wall Street – a German immigrant, very small, very soft spoken. An academic. A total gentleman.

"I was used to walking onto a trading floor and talking with some of the biggest, most imposing traders on Wall Street, people who had a physical presence and booming voices. I just towered over Harry. But immediately, it was

Harry Hutzler, left, and Jon Schoolar formed AIM's version
of "The Odd Couple," a two-man management team on
AIM Weingarten Fund with an average age of 45.

comfortable. He knew how to play the game, not so much for the money, although obviously everyone does. But because it was fun.

"We clicked right away. Julian was a bit more of a loner. I remember flying up to Dallas after I had gotten settled and coming to see him. I had this whole long list of things that I could do for him, having come from a relatively sophisticated shop. He was such a gentleman. He just sat there and listened to me. I had a lot of ideas about how I could help him improve what was going on, not from a stock picking standpoint, but just how to run a department.

"He listened. When I finished, he said, 'That is really fascinating. I appreciate your coming here, but you don't

have to call me. I'm doing just great. I will call you.' And
so forth. Basically, he escorted me out of the office, but
he did it in a very nice way. So I never got as close to
Julian, as a professional, but he was a real nice guy.

"That was our triangle: New York with Harry. Dallas
with Julian. And then AIM here in Houston. Then, in
early 1987, Mr. Bauer called me off the trading desk and
into an office. He said that he wanted someone to go to
New York and find out what Harry does and how he does
it. In short, learn from the master. Would I like to do it? I
just fell over. I was a native Houstonian. But if you wanted
to get ahead in this business, you had to go to New York.
So I had it all.

"I went four times a year, for two or three weeks, during the heaviest earnings periods of the year for us in
terms of trading. We were a little skinny on funds, so I
borrowed a guy's room at the Yale Club, right across from
Grand Central Station, about the size of my office. It was
like $80 a night. If you were going to stay in New York
for two weeks, you couldn't afford the Grand Hyatt.

"I worked with Harry and then I would come home. It
was neat for both of us. Since Harry had run a one-man
shop, he hadn't taken a vacation in 20 years. So Harry cut
loose. He worked with me for one month out of three.
The other two months he would take his wife on a cruise,
or they would go to China or Alaska. They went everywhere. And it gave me a little room to sort of find my
own way."

Until Hutzler retired in 1993, he and Schoolar were a
terrific team, but the oddest of couples. One tall, one
short. One 65, the other 25. "We had a little problem
there," Schoolar says. "So we used to tell people that the
average of our management team was 45.

*Jon Schoolar: The bottom line to successful
equity investing requires a bottom-up approach.*

"In 1988, I happened to take a trip to Kenya. I was
gone for about four weeks and grew my beard. It made
me look five years older. So when I came back, I kept the
beard. Ted Bauer hated it. Despised it. But I said it made
me look 30. And I have to look at least 30 because when
I walk in with Harry people stare, as if I was skipping my
junior high classes."

But as the years progressed, Schoolar made a more
indelible impression on his audiences as the strong performance of the funds he and Hutzler managed continued
to make headlines. One day, Schoolar was doing a
regional meeting for a brokerage house and a doctor in
the audience stood up and said, "I'm going to put a certain amount of money in that fund you're talking about.
But if you come meet my daughter, I'll put a lot more in."

The short version of what Schoolar learned from his
mentor was this: The stock market is not the video game

Julian Lerner, left, and Lanny Sachnowitz have been the only lead portfolio managers in the 32-year history of AIM Charter Fund.

that people make it out to be. The stock market is just the value of the economy, of all the people working out there. And so, over time, it goes up; you have the long run on your side.

In the mid-'80s, most money managers were still using the top-down system. Meaning that they started out by asking, which way is the market going? What does the economy look like? What are interest rates going to do? Given all of that, what stocks should I buy?

Hutzler taught that this was the wrong science because any of the big bets could fail, throwing the whole portfolio out of whack. What Harry taught was bottom-up. This was the Peter Lynch theory, but with more math. That is, go company by company, assemble the ones you really like and don't worry if it is going to rain or shine.

"The analogy I use," said Schoolar, "is to think of an impressionist painting. A pointillist painter, where you put little dabs of paint on the canvas, and if you stand real close to the canvas you don't see a pattern, but when you step away, then you can see, oh, water lilies. Concentrate on each dab of paint. Buy Intel. Buy Compaq. Buy whatever, and the big picture takes care of itself."

Schoolar, like other professional money managers, takes his job very seriously. Those who have worked with successful fund managers, or who have observed them from a distance, realize that it takes a special type of individual to deal with the tremendous responsibility of managing other people's money.

Carol Drawe, who has worked in AIM's Investment Department since 1985, recalls a night when Schoolar was in his office very late. She stopped by to leave something on his desk and jokingly said, "Now, Jon, I hope you're paying attention to what you're doing because you have my life savings in your hands.

"Jon looked up at me and said, with not a trace of a smile, 'Oh, that's not half as bad as what I'm facing someday.' I said, 'What's that?' And he said, 'The next time I go to dinner with my parents, they're going to ask me what I've done with their retirement money. I have to look them in the eye and be able to tell them that they are safe. Do you know what it's like to eat dinner at your parents' home, if you've lost some of their money?'

"Ever since then, I have a whole different view of Jon Schoolar. I've learned to really look behind what the person usually sees, when they are looking at the portfolio manager, when the markets are going crazy and the traders and the managers and the clients are yelling and screaming and hanging up the phone on each other. And they like to do that.

"At one point, we were putting in a new phone system, and there were complaints about that because you couldn't slam the receiver down as loudly and forcefully, and people didn't want to change. So some of them kept the old phones in order to have that dramatic ending to whatever they wanted to end. But deep inside, they have a terrific sense of concern for the people whose money they are dealing with, and they need to balance that with this self-confidence, this ability to say, 'I'm good at this.'

"A lot of times, in the old days, shareholders would call in with questions about the high yield fund. Some of them were little old ladies, who were counting on this money to keep them eating over the next few years of their lives. That puts a certain pressure on people, when they are getting those calls, and the people are asking, 'What have you done with my money?'"

Drawe recalls one call from an irate shareholder that spoke volumes about how quickly AIM Weingarten Fund became a household name in the mutual fund industry. It turns out the caller's husband had such foresight as to have invested $10,000 in the Weingarten Fund years earlier. She was now very comfortable, thanks to that and a couple of other investments. But she was one of those people who liked to stay on top of her investments – as she had every right to do.

"She would call in every day and ask questions and we had started one of the first recorded, automated menus," Drawe says. "And this day, her call was transferred to my extension. She said she did not like the way the message was done. She did not like the voice of the person. She thought the voice was much too soft and hard to hear. Finally, she said, 'Young lady, if I had a fund such as Weingarten, I wouldn't whisper about it. I'd shout!'"

Chapter Eight

BLACK
MONDAY

On October 19, 1987, better known as "Black Monday," the Dow Jones Industrial Average fell 508.32 points to close at 1,738.40, shattering all previous records. The Dow had dropped by 22.6 percent, almost twice the percentage it fell on October 29, 1929, when markets experienced a one-day panic that signaled the onset of the Great Depression. The value of U.S. equities had dropped more than $500 billion in a matter of hours on Black Monday, erasing a significant chunk of a generation's wealth.

"This is a 'good-bye' opportunity," one person on Wall Street joked. "Good-bye house, good-bye car, good-bye bonus." In reality, however, the stock market's precipitous drop indeed represented the buying opportunity of a lifetime and ushered in new era of equity investing only a year after AIM had made its first big splash by purchasing the Weingarten, Constellation, and Charter Funds.

Many believed stock prices were near their limit in late 1987 after a five-year expansion. Hostile takeovers had become commonplace in the 1980s, pushing prices upward. Corporate raiders such as T. Boone Pickens would find a company with a stock believed to be under-valued and attempt to acquire it by issuing high-yield bonds. The cash flow and the value of the company to be acquired provided much of the collateral needed for the bonds. Once the acquisition was completed, new man-agement would dismantle the corporation and sell the assets off in small chunks. The idea was that the company was worth more in little pieces than together. Because corporate raiders needed to acquire enough shares to control the company, they paid a premium for the stock, and takeovers continued to push the market upward.

Another factor that contributed to Black Monday was a relatively new trading concept known as "portfolio insurance." In theory, the strategy would protect an in-vestor from losses in a declining market because users could sell futures contracts that would rise in value if stock prices fell. But the theory had an Achilles' heel. Those who employed the practice of portfolio insurance accelerated the market's drop as selling prompted more selling and the lack of liquidity became a huge problem.

Schoolar had been working with Harry Hutzler for only a few months on the Weingarten and Constellation Funds and was in New York on Black Monday. "It was a hell of a deal," Schoolar says. "We didn't have all of the equipment that we had in Houston and Harry's office was just one small room. We had a Dow Jones tape ticker that spilled out on the floor and up to our knees. We were afraid, and depressed, like a lot of people in the business.

*Ted Bauer reassured AIM employees of their job security during
the market's record-setting, one-day drop in October 1987.*

We worried we were going to get redeemed, that our
fund was going to go away. We wouldn't have money to
pay the shareholders.

"So the thing I did that day was just to say, 'Let's try
and make as much money as we can today and worry
about tomorrow when it gets here.' Some stocks were
down 40 points. We were buying those. Some were down
10. We were selling those. We couldn't even make the
paper match up at the end of the day, you know, what I
had bought and sold. I didn't have any of my stuff."

The Dow dropped 9 percent in the first 90 minutes
and remained about 200 points down from the opening
bell until midafternoon. Ted Bauer's son-in-law, Andy

Mary Gentempo, now in charge of AIM Fund Services' financial service department, was in charge of AIM's telephone and processing group on Black Monday.

Hartman, was in Houston that day on a business trip to learn how to manage high-yield bonds. Bauer recalls how a selling frenzy triggered by computer sell programs drove the market down another 300 points by the end of the session. "The SEC called me up and asked what was going on," Bauer said. "And I said, 'Not much. The brokers stand between our shareholders and us. It took us so long to get this company going that we're tough as nails.'"

Meanwhile, Schoolar was exhausted from an emotionally draining day. He realized he couldn't operate out of New York, so he caught the Red Eye back to Houston. As it happened, Kathy Whitmire, then the mayor of Houston, was seated one or two rows behind Schoolar with her entourage.

"I was sprawled in my seat, drained, and thinking, 'My gosh! What does this mean? How are my parents positioned? What are we going to do?' All of this is going through my head and behind me I hear some aide say to

Kathy Whitmire, 'Did you hear, Mayor? The market fell 508 points today!'

"And she said, 'Oh, my.' That was all. I remember thinking, 'Oh, my?' For this calamity? And I realized, apparently there were people in the world who didn't live and die by the Dow Jones Averages.

"We got into the office early the next morning and made all sorts of plans for the market to just collapse again, and it didn't. The highlight of the day was mid-morning, when Mr. Bauer went to every department, to every desk, and said basically the same thing: 'AIM is in great shape. We don't have lavish offices. We don't borrow a lot of money. No one's job is in jeopardy. So concentrate on doing the best job that you can do today and don't worry about your situation.' That was exactly the right thing to say."

Judy Creel, AIM's director of corporate resources, recalls how teamwork helped the company get through a difficult time. "We talked about how to reduce expenses. It even reached the point where someone said, 'The printer gives me one blank sheet before it starts printing. If we can do away with the blank sheet, how much can we save?' Thankfully, in a couple of days the market turned the other way and we didn't have to circle the wagons. We didn't think about laying off any employees."

Dawn Hawley had just been hired by AIM when Black Monday made her second-guess her decision. "I didn't have a clue about how much this company depended on the stock market. But you can imagine how my head was spinning. The day I started with the company, the first piece of mail in my in-box was the resignation of the guy who had hired me, and then exactly two weeks later the market dropped 500 points.

"The next morning, my husband was shaving, and I remember sitting on the edge of the bathtub and telling him, 'We may have made a bad decision here. My boss quit the day before I started, the market dropped 508 points, I have no job description, and I am in a brand new job.' I didn't know what to expect."

Even some of AIM's wholesalers were concerned. Two of them quit the next day thinking AIM wouldn't survive the market's calamity. "But the Federal Reserve came in and saved the market," Bauer recalled. "The Fed deserves a lot of credit for the swift action it took."

Federal Reserve Chairman Alan Greenspan was so concerned about the looming possibility of a financial crisis that he convened the first of a series of daily conference calls with other members of the Fed board and officials at the 12 Federal Reserve banks the Friday before Black Monday. "I think we're playing it on a day-to-day basis," Greenspan told his colleagues. "And in a crisis environment, I suspect we shouldn't really focus on longer-term policy questions until we get beyond this period of immediate chaos."

Greenspan believed that maintaining liquidity was the primary way the Fed could contain the resulting damage from Black Monday. Investors and securities firms needed to borrow huge amounts to meet obligations such as margin calls, and Greenspan assured banks and other financial firms that the Fed would supply enough cash to prevent any liquidity squeeze.

Given the benefit of hindsight, many economists believe Black Monday was a blessing. Why? Because it relieved so many pressures that had built up in the U.S. economy in the mid-1980s that might have forced the

Gary Beauchamp, AIM's economic strategist, was manager of the Associated Planners Government Securities Fund for AIM in October 1987.

Fed to raise interest rates so high that it might have caused an economic slump.

Another positive aspect of Black Monday was the way it eventually changed America's outlook on equities at a time AIM needed to shift attention away from fixed-income and toward its three new equity funds. Investors came to realize that stock prices rise as companies grow and prices eventually reach excess levels that prompt healthy corrections. Despite the '87 crash, the market was actually up a couple of percentage points for the year. And had investors bought stock the day before the crash, they'd have logged about a 300-percent gain since then, according to the Dow Jones Industrial Average. The bottom-line lesson: Investors who buy and hold for the long term will be rewarded.

The shift in investor sentiment, however, wasn't sudden. AIM Limited Maturity Treasury Shares, a conservative fund built by laddering one- and two-year treasury notes, was the biggest thing that kept AIM wholesalers in front of financial advisors for the following year. AIM knew it needed to find a way to trumpet the long-term advantage of equities and capitalize on the fact that Black Monday, indeed, was a "good buy" opportunity.

Chapter Nine

THE CASE FOR
EQUITIES

Jim Salners, one of the first six wholesalers hired by AIM in 1986 to promote its new line of equity funds, had taken his show on the road. He had scheduled a breakfast meeting and was eager to talk to 20 members of American Capital's Memphis office about Weingarten, Constellation, and Charter. "I had gone out and bought a big box of doughnuts and some bagels and walked in with cartons of orange juice and the like," Salners said. "They'd consumed almost all of those before I got up to speak.

"I started talking about the Weingarten Fund, and about six or seven of them stood up, pushed back their seats, and walked toward the door. I shouted, 'Hey, wait a minute! I mean…you ate my doughnuts! At least listen to my story!" And one of them said, 'Well, we would…but we thought this was American Insured Mortgage!' In those days, that happened a lot. They just didn't know who we were."

Although AIM was still in the midst of an identity crisis among financial advisors in 1986, the company was emphatic in its decision to sell its funds through third-party intermediaries and not directly to the general public. AIM has always adhered to the philosophy that financial advisors perform a very valuable service to investors, and that many investors have neither the time nor the expertise to make decisions based solely on information provided by financial publications and other sources. Instead, many investors want an analysis of their unique personal needs and objectives from a professional before making a decision.

As a result, Ted Bauer believed a mutual fund company had to meet three requirements in order to successfully penetrate the broker/dealer market: it must have products with attractive performance in a full family of funds; it must have acceptance of the product line by the "home office" of the broker/dealer; and it must offer a high level of service to the individual salesman. AIM was prepared to deliver on all three counts, and Salners was determined to be called something other than the guy who brought the bagels. But it was an uphill climb.

"The reason people were down on equities was because we had just come out of a decade where equities didn't go anywhere because interest rates were very high," he recalls. "But I found out that 70 to 75 percent of the people who bought bond funds reinvested their dividends. So, when I went to do a public seminar, I would ask, 'What do you really want out of this investment?' People would invariably say they wanted their money to grow. To me, that said people were investing in the wrong thing. If they wanted growth, they should be investing in the equity markets."

*Jim Salners, left, hoped he wouldn't become a laughingstock
when interviewing with Ted Bauer for a job as a wholesaler.*

Fixed-income products were still extremely popular in
1986 and 1987. Equities, by comparison, were a very difficult sell. AIM had not yet become a household name in
terms of equity funds and Salners was knocking on doors
in nine states and three time zones. It was a tough job for
a former thespian who had been trained as a chemical
engineer and landed a job as a wholesaler at AIM in
September 1986 after oil prices had plummeted.

"I had two choices: poverty or go to work at AIM," Salners says. "I had guys telling me I should be a salesman, but I was trained as a chemical engineer. I kept asking myself, 'Why should I be a salesman?' And Ted Bauer saw right through me. 'What do you do,' he asked, 'if oil goes back to $35 a barrel?' But I was fortunate in that I was quick on my feet and articulate. I was hired in September of '86. Right after I got the job, I attended a training session with AIM's other five wholesalers and everybody at the table was talking about their securities licenses. I said, 'Hey, I've got a Texas driver's license!'

"My wife helped me prepare for the exam to get my license. She was quizzing me. The first question was, 'What's a mutual fund?' I said, 'Let's go to the next question."

Salners' first boss at AIM was Jeffrey Hyde, an Englishman. Jack Pohlemus was the first wholesaler hired, and helped put together the original staff. Pohlemus and Salners had worked together at an oil company for about five years. "Two weeks after I started at AIM, one wholesaler died of a heart attack," Salners recalled. "The next week, Jeffrey quit. He had been using the job at AIM as a stepping stone, trying to get back to London. He went to work for Alliance in New York."

Hyde's replacement was Wayne Leizear, a wholesaler who became AIM's national sales manager. Leizear tried to commute between New York and Houston, but resigned as national sales manager after one year and ended up becoming AIM's wholesaler in New York. Forrest Pragoff, also one of AIM's original six wholesalers, replaced Leizear for one year until Mike Cemo was hired as director of marketing in the fall of 1988. Cemo then promoted Salners to national sales manager.

"The six of us went in different directions in terms of trying to make things work," Salners said. "I started with E.F. Hutton and they opened their arms a little bit; Merrill Lynch as well. We started out like a house afire by the middle of 1987, then the fall was a disaster after Black Monday. When Mike came to AIM in 1988 and interviewed me for the job as national sales manager, he said, 'I don't know why, but I think you can do this.' But after I became national sales manager, I still had a difficult time hiring people."

Salners recalled an important factor that proved critical to AIM's long-term success. "In the mid-'80s, other firms were selling government-plus bonds like crazy," he said. "This was the first of many of the black eyes for the fund business, using derivatives, which had not been used up to that time. It was like wrapping the American flag around your prospectus and selling it as a Godsend with a 16-percent return, even as rates were falling rapidly.

"I went to Ted Bauer and Gary Crum and told them, 'We're getting killed out there! Why can't we come out with a government-plus fund?' They went through the math with me, why it was destined to fail. They showed everybody why it wouldn't work. That became part of our philosophy – stick to our knitting."

While others were sifting through the rubble of the market's nosedive in October 1987, Salners and other AIM wholesalers came up with an innovative way to transform the situation into a competitive advantage. Crum recalls how Merrill Lynch had just changed its broker reporting and accounting system and the brokers had the ability to run screens of specific funds.

"It was a totally new system to the Merrill Lynch broker," Crum says. "Jim went in and learned how to operate the

*Members of AIM's sales force at a 1995 wholesalers' meeting:
Left to right, Gordon Sprague, Steve Gregory, Wayne Leizear,
Larry Manierre, Doug O'Dell, Bob Cherichella, Jim Salners,
and Buzz Parker next to Ted Bauer.*

Merrill system and then educated them how to run it as he was traveling around the country. He would show consultants that when you looked under the 'growth' category on the computer, Weingarten Equity Fund would come up as the No. 1 fund."

Salners used the same strategy at every Merrill Lynch office he visited. He'd go to the computer and show reps how he could select a screen of all growth funds available to sell at Merrill Lynch. Then he'd narrow the list to those funds that had a cumulative return of at least 100 percent in the previous five years. Then he'd narrow the list to those remaining funds that had a return of at least 10 percent in the previous year. "You'd hit 'Enter' and 'Boom!' the computer would list Weingarten right at the top," Salners said. The computer demonstration, plus the Case for Equities, proved a successful one-two punch for AIM.

"It was the end of the '80s and everybody wanted to be in the industry and part of the problem was Merrill had taken on a lot of young retail brokers," Crum said. "The average Merrill broker had been there only a short while, and been fully educated on how to sell common stocks. So we were responsible for educating a whole new generation of brokers on how to sell common stock."

AIM showed the retail brokerage houses it was in the market through thick and thin with the wholesalers' support of the brokerage house retail branches in 1987 and 1988. As Ted Bauer likes to say, there is no acceptance by the industry of a firm that is intermittent in its effort. Although equity sales remained low during that period, brokers were learning the AIM story. And when equity fund sales returned, AIM would be the beneficiary.

As AIM wholesalers traveled throughout the country after the '87 crash, they realized it would take substantial evidence to convince financial advisors to move investors out of fixed-income products and into stocks. After all, bonds had produced unusually robust returns since the 1970s, and equity investing had been rocked by a harsh bear market in 1973-74 and by a one-day, 22 percent drop in October 1987. People were afraid of the inherent risks of the equity markets, fears that were well-placed if investors focused solely on short-term results.

The primary thrust of AIM's sales efforts in the late 1980s was based on a simple, yet compelling story that illustrated the potential long-term rewards of investing in stocks. "The Case for Equities" would serve as a foundation for AIM's fund sales for more than a decade and helped position the company to benefit from the bull market of the 1990s. It illustrated how stocks had significantly outperformed bonds through a variety of market conditions and how a long-term approach to investing through equity mutual funds could significantly reduce exposure to potentially volatile results.

One classic historical study became the cornerstone for AIM's equity sales presentation. A simple bar chart showed how a $100 investment in the S&P 500 at the end of 1925 would have grown to more than $60,000 by 1988. By contrast, a $100 investment in long-term bonds would have grown to approximately $2,000 over the same time period. And by 2000, those figures had become even more demonstrative, as a $100 investment in equities would have grown to more than $250,000 compared to approximately $5,000 in long-term bonds.

The Case for Equities was a particularly powerful message when used to illustrate the importance of investing in stocks in order to save for retirement as the Baby Boom generation became concerned about the long-term stability of the Social Security system. AIM's sales force emphasized the point that investing in equities was the best way to save for retirement, especially given the effects of taxes and inflation.

Wholesalers were quick to mention that if an individual's combined federal and state tax rate was 40 percent and inflation averaged 6 percent annually, an investment would need to generate a 10 percent total return for the individual to maintain his or her current purchasing

*Jim Salners used The Case for Equities to help prompt wholesale changes
in the way equity mutual funds were sold. Salners is director of sales
strategy and planning for AIM's Retail Marketing Department.*

power. The only way to accomplish that, from a historical
perspective, was to invest in equities.

The Case for Equities began paying off for AIM in
1988 when the company was one of the few mutual fund
complexes to experience a growth in net assets under
management – from $9 billion to $12 billion. Armed with
three new equity funds and a tremendous sales pitch, all
AIM needed was a timely opportunity to reach a large
number of prospective investors and take a quantum leap
in the fund business. The opportunity finally presented
itself in late 1989, when Salners and Leizear were having
lunch in New York with Merrill's East Coast manager.

"Weingarten had been in *Money* magazine's performance charts every month for 18 to 24 months," Salners
said. "A very strong article described our style of managing, and said our fund performance was at a peak. The fel-

low from Merrill asked, 'What are you guys doing in January?' I looked at Wayne and said, 'Anything you want!'

"Another fund was going to be a featured fund in their system, and then backed out, and they needed a replacement. They said, 'Maybe we ought to do the AIM Weingarten Fund.' Jon Schoolar, Mike Cemo, and I met with their folks about a month later and made the arrangements on how we were going to promote it. Harry Hutzler, Jon and I flew up on New Year's Day to prepare a video broadcast to their entire system. Bob Mulholland was the host.

"We did the broadcast that afternoon, taped it in a little studio, put on makeup, the whole bit. We ended up visiting 22 cities in 28 days. That marketing effort put us on the map, really, for the first time. We did $100 million in sales in January and today that would be a third of a good week. Then we did the Constellation Fund that summer, and followed it with Charter. We never looked back from that time forward."

Under the direction of Cemo, who joined AIM as president of retail marketing in 1988, AIM followed with a blitzkrieg in which every wholesaler called on every Merrill Lynch office for 30 days. The idea was not only to sell as much AIM Weingarten Fund as possible, but also to get every wholesaler's name on the books and get a ticket from that office. AIM was successful in 485 of 517 Merrill Lynch offices.

"Mike was able to bring his connections in the broker/ dealer community, which I think are monumental, when he joined AIM, and that's one of the keys to opening the door," said Lou Harvey, president of DALBAR, a Boston-based independent mutual fund monitor. "You don't get into Merrill's system because you have a slick brochure or a compelling argument. It's all about relationships."

At about the same time, AIM's sales force began pushing a unit trust product called Government Securities Equity Trust to Prudential offices with the idea of breaking down walls and getting on brokers' books. GSET was a combination of U.S. government zero-coupon bonds and shares of AIM Weingarten Fund. The selling idea was based on the concept that the bonds would appreciate to the value of a shareholder's original investment in 10 years and the value of AIM Weingarten Fund shares at the end of the 10-year period would be a plus.

"We went from $250 million in sales the year before, to $500 million in 1990, then to $2.5 billion," Salners said. "By 1991, Merrill Lynch told us the Case for Equities had been responsible for a 50 percent increase in equity sales in the mutual fund industry. A few years ago, we started a Billionaires Club for salesmen who had achieved that much in sales, and we gave away five plaques. The next year, we had to start adding a diamond because some of them were selling $2 billion.

"Today, AIM is recognized as one of the premier players in the industry. Underlining all of this, the funds have been strong and have made a lot of money. One of the great pleasures I take in going around the country today is meeting the people who years ago walked out on our presentations."

Chapter Ten

MARKETING
MAGIC

AIM had been able to gain a foothold in the equity fund market with its acquisition of the Weingarten, Constellation, and Charter Funds in 1986. But having good products is only part of the battle. To become truly successful, a mutual fund company also must have a superb sales force and outstanding customer service.

The fact that Weingarten Fund had the best 10-year record of any growth fund on the Merrill Lynch screen gave AIM instant access to the nation's biggest mutual fund sales machine. At the time, AIM's Retail Marketing Department consisted of six field wholesalers, 12 staffers in the home office, and a revolving door at the top. Ted Bauer knew he needed to find the right man to jump-start AIM's equity sales with the stock market still trying to recover from Black Monday. Bauer's search ended only a few miles from AIM's Greenway Plaza offices when he invited Mike Cemo for an interview.

*Status cymbal: Mike Cemo during his days
as a rock band drummer in the 1960s.*

Cemo was a native Houstonian, the son of a barber and an alumnus of St. Thomas High School. He graduated from the University of Houston after changing his major from chemical engineering to economics. Cemo had started his career in the industry in 1971 as an assistant in the marketing department at Houston-based American Capital, which later became Van Kampen American Capital. American Capital had been spun off by American General Insurance, a training ground for several AIM employees.

Cemo worked his way up to vice president at American Capital, and then spent three years in the home office. He later worked two years in the field and became

the firm's top producer. Cemo was promoted to national
sales manager and senior vice president in 1978 at the age
of 32. In eight years under Cemo's direction, American
Capital increased its assets under management from $2
billion to $19 billion.

Dawn Hawley, AIM's chief financial officer, recalls
the day Cemo first met with Bauer in August 1988. "I
could hear this wild man talking, and he was down the
hall, interviewing with Ted. There was a personal computer standing alone further down the hall, in a corner.
Of course, we didn't have the Internet then or all the
fancy gadgets. Mike wanted to show Ted some kind of
sales program that he had developed.

"Now, Mike talks as fast and as loud as I do. My excuse
is, I'm from New York, but Mike was born here in
Houston, so I don't know where he gets his speaking
style. So I remember this guy coming in and I can hear
him all the way down in my office. He's saying to Ted,
'Let me show you this,' and he's doing the whole pitch.
That was Mike. And that was a milestone because he put
in our marketing program. He put a plan together and it
took about a year to build up a sales force, then get out
there and push Weingarten, Constellation, and Charter. I
still remember him feeding his programs into the computer."

Cemo's reputation as a wild man began about the time
he started to play drums in a band called The Six Pents as
a student in the '60s. The band was composed of four
friends who hooked up during their high school days at
St. Thomas. The group released six records and opened
shows for the likes of the Lovin' Spoonfuls and Herman's
Hermits. But music wasn't really Cemo's first love.

*Mike Cemo and Ringo Starr had one thing
in common — they both played drums.*

"I did it to get girls," he says. "I mowed yards until I
got enough money to buy my first drum. My friend, John
Bonno, who is my CPA now, decided to play bass. We
had a crazy, ugly guy named Roger Romano, who played
lead, who ended up being Doctor Rocket and is still in
the business today. We made records, changed names,
had wonderful times.

"We had four-part harmony and did all of the Beatles
and Beach Boys stuff. The best year my dad ever had as a
barber was when he made five grand. The first year the
band's record came out, when I was just starting at UH
and living at home, we made $15,000 apiece. Working on
weekends, I made three times what my dad made in a
year. I bought a beautiful, blue 1966 Corvette.

"I had most of my clothes ripped off at a couple of gigs. We were invited one night to Keys Auditorium, in Corpus Christi, to open for a national group. We were showing our new image and our British sound for the first time. We were dressed up in our fruit boot outfits, with our little Beatle boots, and just looked awful. We had brand new amplifiers.

"The curtains open and in front of the stage 5,000 kids are on their feet. No chairs. It's a dance concert. We had never seen one of these before. Beautiful auditorium. We started with our first song, which was, 'Hard Day's Night,' which starts with this flam and this big sound. I had drum mikes – one of the first guys in Houston to have them.

"We hit a chord and the sound just about wiped out the first few rows. It melted them. We played six songs. We finished our set. I remember looking out over the crowd as the police lines broke down, and the crowd climbed onto the stage, and the stage manager is hollering, 'Run for the cars! We'll take care of your equipment!

"Six little girls had Romano by the legs. They were pulling him like a wishbone. He had a big old nose, looked like Ringo Starr. They pulled his shoes off. They were ripping at his hair. We got him away, ran for the cars, jumped into a limo and raced to the hotel.

"Boy, that was ecstasy! We got to the hotel and Romano had a ring on his finger that somebody had slipped on. Some little girl. One of those friendship rings. His finger turned black. He couldn't get it off. We literally had to cut it off with a hacksaw. We got rave reviews and that started us off. We were all in college, the only non-drug group around.

Mike Cemo during his tenure as sales chieftain at American Capital.

"We played for three years and it was great. Then, one day, I just woke up, about to graduate, and knew I was not good enough as a drummer. I mean, I could do it, but not well enough to be a professional. The band was transcending again to another name. They ended up being called, 'The Funny Games Commission,' and I told them, 'I'm gone.' I walked down to the garage and looked at my red sparkle probe, my double bass drum set, and said, 'Now, if you are going to transcend, you are going to transcend.' I sold it the next day and walked away from it. It hurt. It hurt for a long time."

In his second year in college, Cemo went into a school-work program and landed a job as an engineering aide at Monsanto Chemical. The work paid well, but the real value was in convincing him that he should switch to economics. He stopped just short of a master's degree, but had a huge math background from his engineering courses.

Cemo wanted to land a job as a bond analyst, but he had a time constraint. The Vietnam War was raging and when he called his draft board, and asked how he was doing on the list, a cheery, female voice said, "Oh, you're the first guy to go next month. Congratulations, Mike!"

He put aside thoughts of dialing for dollars. He had 30 days to find a teaching job and qualify for a draft exemption. He called every school district in the city, and finally connected with an administrator at Smiley High School in northeast Houston. "I said, 'My name is Mike Cemo. You don't know me, but I just graduated from college. I thought you might have a teaching position. I can teach chemistry, physics, algebra and, if you have a calculus course, I can teach that to your advanced classes.' "He said, 'Did you say chemistry? Come on down!'

Cemo went to interview for the job on a Saturday morning. The process didn't take long.

"Mike, do you *really* teach chemistry?"

"I have 24 hours of credit in organic," Cemo said. "I majored at one time in chemical engineering. I can do that. I can also teach physics. I have nine hours of advanced physics."

"You're hired!"

"Don't you want to see my diploma?"

"No," the administrator said, "let's not clutter this up with technical things."

The semester started on Monday. "It was a wonderful place," Cemo said. "There was no air conditioning. Smiley,

A team approach has worked for AIM in retail marketing, as well as portfolio management. Left to right, retail marketing support manager B.J. Thompson, Mike Cemo, FID national sales manager Mike Vessels, and former IIDD national sales manager Gordon Sprague, who is a senior partner with AMVESCAP.

which was an all-Anglo school, had just integrated with T.C. Elmore, which had been an African-American school. I had 12 kids in my physics class and 40 in each of my four chemistry classes. No laboratory. No books. Nothing. It took us two weeks to get an order filled for the textbooks. I went out to Dow Chemical and got them to donate the glassware and we built our own lab."

Mike loved teaching and, in his brief tenure, may have set a scholastic record for inspiring interest among his students in the reactions of certain chemical mixtures. "This was a great time in my life," he says. "We evacuated the entire school one day because of my class. They loved it. We chlorinated them!

"We were doing our normal dumb experiments with yellow liquids and green liquids, and stuff, and they were learning a few things. I said, 'Tell you what. You have been complaining about these experiments being dull. If we have at least an 85 average in every class at the next test, we will do an absolute, knock down, hurt-your-body type experiment right out of the college chemistry books.

"Man, everybody studied. Every one of the classes made the cut. So we did the chlorine distillation experiment. The first day, we made our glassware. The second day, we took hydrochloric acid and put it over zinc to displace chlorine gas. We caught the chlorine in gas bottles by water displacement.

"When the first class tried it, the exhaust hood failed and we had to evacuate the entire west side of the school. Then, the next day, we took the chlorine gas in their bottles, corked it up real good, and lit it with a hydrogen gas generator. You weren't supposed to have any oxygen in your glass because if you did, it's like the same combustion that blew up the dirigibles. It's a halogen. It explodes like crazy.

"I'm in my classroom and the guys are getting set up. I had talked Dow into giving us chest protectors, pads, hand-to-shoulder gloves, and full-face masks. The kids are in the laboratory talking and putting these things together, using forceps. It was wild. There were three guys acting as observers and one as the chemist in each team of four. Then I hear this explosion go off. It sounds like a 12-gauge shotgun.

"I said, 'Oh, my God! I'm thinking, 'There's going to be blood everywhere!' I ran to the other side of the laboratory and there's this kid who's sitting there with this astonished look on his face. He'd blown everything off the desk and onto the floor. The glass bottle is stuck in the ceiling tiles. All of the guys that were observing are lying on the floor, with their arms over their heads, covered up. The kid said, 'What the heck happened?'

"I said, 'Let me look at your gas bottles.' He'd put a two-hole stopper in each bottle instead of a regular stopper. So oxygen was in there and it was like a hand grenade. The kids loved it! They just loved it! Now every class wanted to get this experiment. It was the greatest motivator you had ever seen. All day, the students were coming up to me and saying, 'Mr. Cemo, is it *really* true that you blew up the whole lab table in your last class?"

"I said, 'Yeah, it was great!'"

Cemo taught for three more years, the last two at Strake Jesuit College Preparatory, a high school in west Houston. He was passed over in the draft lottery and decided the time had come to find his calling. His experiences as a musician and a chemistry teacher had surely prepared him for anything as combustible as the financial markets. That's when Cemo started as a gofer at American Capital.

The American General Capital Funds were acquired by Gerry Tsai (pronounced sigh), a gentleman of Chinese descent, who ran a company called American Can and would soon become a legendary figure in the industry. "If you look him up," says Cemo, "you will find that this is a guy who's never lost money. I've never seen him make a bad trade. He bought the company for $39 million. The first year it paid a $50 million dividend. By then, I was on the board of American Capital and senior vice president for sales. I went to him and said, 'Gerry,

Tad Niederriter, left, accepts one of the four Top Gun Awards he has received from Ted Bauer and Mike Cemo as AIM's most prolific wholesaler.

you ought to take this thing public for 20 percent so you can revalue it.' He sold 20 percent for $78 million and, in two weeks, the remaining shares were worth $400 million.

"The shares of American Can moved up 16 percent because of what happened within the subsidiary. Two years later, in 1984, his $39 million investment was worth $500 million and Gerry Tsai looked like the Wizard of Wall Street. He moved to Hong Kong and became known as the Rockefeller of Asia."

In time, as so frequently happens, a change at the highest level of his company left Mike Cemo with that dangling feeling. He had known Ted Bauer during his years as head of investments at American General, and Mike had been on the sales side.

"I called Ted," he related, "and I said, 'Ted, I heard yesterday from your headhunter that you are looking for a head of sales. I've resigned from the company, cashed out everything that I can here. I don't want to leave Houston. I have plenty of money, but I would like to have a challenge. You're the only act in town. Would you like to talk to me?' He said he really would, and I went to see him.

"I was in a halfway distraught state. After 18 years with a company, it's like a divorce, like losing all of your friends real quick. I walk in and here's this man that I know, but not well. You talk about a nice person. I had already resigned. I didn't play the game well. But I said, 'If I go to work for somebody, I want a piece of the action, but I would like to buy it.'

"Ted said, 'Well, let's put a deal together.' He cut me the fairest two-year guaranteed deal you could imagine. He let me buy five percent of the company, and so I went to my little office on the 19th floor. This whole company at that time consisted of 160 people on the 19th floor. That was in 1988."

When Cemo arrived at AIM, there was no viable sales literature. A home office telemarketing operation was non-existent. The mailroom was two people with a tape dispenser. The AIM Funds were not on the preferred list of any brokers. At the time, AIM had very limited access to key national accounts around the country. One of Cemo's first moves was to hire Patti Hefley, who has been his executive secretary at American Capital.

"One day, Ted came to my office and said, 'Are you ready to go?' I said, 'Yeah, but I've been looking through everything and I can't believe what I see. You've got major problems here. Your sales charge is wrong. Your wholesalers are not working. You have four guys that are incompetent. Do you really want me to do this?'

"He said, 'Absolutely! We need you to get this done. We bought the Weingarten, Constellation, and Charter Funds on a loan. In another year, we're going to start paying principal and interest, instead of interest only. If you don't get these funds sold, and these assets built, I don't know what will happen.'

"I thought, 'Gee, nobody had mentioned any of this.' I sat down. I really dug into it. I looked at all the possibilities. And I just got depressed. About three days later, I'm in my office and near tears. Here I was: on the board of directors of a very old, established company, making huge bucks. Maybe I should not have been so impatient. I hadn't been with AIM a week and I was already second-guessing myself."

Cemo knew changes – big changes – had to be made. In some ways, he felt like The Sweeper, the guy in the mob movies who comes in after a shootout, disposes of the bodies, and cleans up all the evidence.

"Ted is the kind of guy," he said, "who wouldn't fire anybody unless the guy had stepped way, way over the line or something. He really tried to work things out and I was that way, too. But here I was confronted with just an absolutely awesome task. I didn't know what to do. We had no systems, no literature, no people. I mean, nothing...except these three beautiful funds with great track records, the no-load funds Ted had the wisdom to buy.

"Basically, we had two operations – and we still do. We had the money market operation that sells to the trust department of the large banks, and that had about $10 billion. It was making about $8 million in cash flow a year. That was the cash cow. But it was not a lot of return on $10 billion. Only eight basis points.

Mike Cemo's three keys of success in mutual fund marketing —
superior performance, wide distribution, and quality client service.

"Then there was this group, the one I was taking over. At that time, we had $300 million in there in retail funds and another $300 million in a fund called Summit Contractual, and that was it. So a total of maybe $600 million on my side.

"I'm sitting there," Cemo went on, "and Ted walked in and asked, 'What's the matter? I said, 'Ted, this is just incredible.' He raised a hand and said, 'Calm down. We have confidence in you. You *will* get it done. You have time. We have time. We are not going to make any changes. Just do what you have to do." I looked at him and I thought, 'You know, this is a truly good guy. I told myself, 'I'm going to make this thing work for this guy.'

"Here was my problem. I had made all of my money selling through brokerage houses. That was all we did at American Capital. My biggest client was Merrill Lynch. So at AIM, we wanted a structured organization that would do the same thing. We had the contacts. We had the product, somewhat questionable because it was new to us, but the records were good. We were really coming out of the box, starting from scratch. At least, we felt like it was speculative. I mean, a lot of companies tried to do this kind of thing and didn't make it. We were lucky in many ways. We were lucky in that we were equity-oriented in a market that was about to break out.

"We had just gotten to the end of the 1988 calendar, the market had dropped 25 percent, and it didn't look good at that point. What we didn't know was that the market was about to have a wonderful ride, almost pure bliss. We thanked God for it. You need to be willing to accept good luck, and we never disillusioned ourselves about that. That helps a lot if you want to build a company.

"In the first phase, we basically lost two or three wholesalers. I looked at their compensation. They were all being given a guarantee of $140,000 a year against a draw of $2,000 per month. Which meant that they had to sell $70 million before they got a bonus. But they had this big, up-front deal. All eight salesmen also were doing less than $150 million combined. Some territories were doing $15 million or less. We had guys with golf handicaps that you would not believe. We had guys shooting a two-handicap! That's a great way to tell if your salespeople are working. If someone has a two-handicap, you have a major problem.

"I called everyone in and I said, 'I have bad news and good news. The bad news is that your field trip into Disneyland is over and your new salary is $70,000 a year. The good news is that you get bonused from Day One. So if you sell $10 million, we give you a check for $20 grand. If you sell $50 million, we give you $100,000. So now you have an incentive to stop playing golf and go to work. I hope that doesn't cause you too much trouble with your personal schedules, but this is it.' The guys were great. We ended up with eight wholesalers and had to hire a few new guys. Doug O'Dell and Buzz Parker and a bunch of others stayed and over the last 10 years these funds made millionaires out of 20 of them.

"We went out and attacked the market. We went after Merrill Lynch, and then we went after Prudential, then PaineWebber. We built that division, got it up to about $300 million in sales. But they were good sales, at the right numbers. We were making enough to pay our bills.

"Ted had given me a $4 million loss budget. We never had to take all of it. We were able to stay under that and now we were up to about $1 billion in assets. We were generating about $6 million in revenue, which was almost as much as the other side of the firm."

Under Cemo, AIM's retail business began to blossom. The company turned in a $12 million profit, which increased the following year to $18 million. Retail assets climbed to $1.5 billion. They rolled out new products and opened two new sales channels. They hired marketing specialists and introduced high-quality marketing literature. Today, AIM Distributors, the retail marketing subsidiary of AIM Management Group, has more than 600 employees under Mike Cemo, the former drummer and teacher.

Cemo is fond of comparing a mutual fund to a stool with three legs. "One leg is money management, which is Gary Crum's group," he says. "They sit around all day making huge decisions about what to buy and sell.

"The second leg is marketing and distribution. We are wholesalers, meaning that we do not sell directly to anybody. We do it through a third party. If you wanted to buy a fund today, I would give you the name of a broker to help you. It makes for an extremely efficient operation because I don't have brick and mortar. Merrill Lynch has, and I rent theirs.

"The third leg is shareholder services. It has a transfer agency that Jack Caldwell ran prior to his retirement. Jack just came in and saved us. In the early days, we didn't have very many trades going through, maybe 200 a day, if we were lucky. Well, now we make 20,000 trades and have over 6 million shareholders to service, and that's a lot of work.

"It isn't enough that you continue to grow all three legs. You must grow them in a balanced manner. If you grow one leg faster than the others, the stool falls over."

When Cemo was presented with the mutual fund industry's award as Marketer of the Year in 1996, it was a powerful moment of recognition for the man and the company. It confirmed the fact that this had been another brilliant piece of corporate matchmaking. And it erased any doubt that both had arrived.

"We have our share of small problems, but on balance this is a unique company," Cemo says. "We don't lose a lot of people here. When they come, they want to stay. I think they see the future. They all know that we are going to take this battle all the way. They want to go along for the ride.

"The question is, can we really make it in the big leagues? Can we go to that next level and play the game? That's what gets you up every morning and gets our blood going. We want to go out there and take a swing at it."

Chapter Eleven

SAFETY, LIQUIDITY, AND YIELD

Although AIM had begun to generate consider-able attention with its rapidly growing retail fund business in the 1990s, the institutional marketplace remained a significant contributor to the company's bottom line. Institutional money market funds had been AIM's bread and butter long before the huge increase in popularity of equity mutual funds among the general public. Among the reasons for AIM's success with institutional investors was its reputation for providing quality products and services with low fees.

"The fact our fees were so low enabled us to buy the highest-quality paper," Ted Bauer said. "Our funds had the shortest average maturity in the business. We were able to convince people that they could give up a little yield to pay our fees because we had a whole team of people who were managing nothing but money market funds. In a bank, they might get some people who weren't specialists. At one point, more than 50 percent of the trust profits at First City National Bank of Houston came from our money market funds. They made more money than we did."

But it was still difficult, at times, for AIM to convince firms to do business with its institutional division. Bauer cited an example of how Valley National Bank wouldn't invest in AIM's money market funds until members of its management team visited the Houston operation, which was rather undistinguished because the fledgling company was still using rented tables. Indeed, all 16 of AIM's employees knew one another on a first-name basis. The company simply was trying to grow its $125 million in assets under management when Bauer first talked to Abbott Sprague about joining AIM's institutional team. Today, Sprague is president of Fund Management Company and the top man in AIM's institutional department that oversees more than $40 billion in assets.

A native of Rhode Island, Sprague had plunged into the investment business in 1978, straight out of Bowdoin College. In a sense, he was born into it. The Sprague family owned a bank in Maine and, perhaps as an early recognition of his talents, Abbott was the only family member allowed to work there, during his summer vacations through his freshman year in college.

"My grandfather had always given me bits and pieces of stock," Sprague says, "so the interest was there. I was a teller and a loan officer. They used to send me to all of the branches that had been recently robbed. That was always nerve-wracking. I was one of the few male tellers they had, and the bank tried to get me into repo – repossession – work. That wasn't fun, so I didn't last long.

When he first joined the company, Abbott Sprague had no idea he'd eventually become an institution of sorts during a 20-year career at AIM.

"In college, I majored in history archeology, but I was appointed to the school's investment committee. They had about $30 million in funds, and in the 1970's that was relatively large. That was what really kicked me into gear to decide what I ought to be doing. I wanted to manage money. That meant fixed-income because interest rates were rising. Inflation was coming in. Bonds seemed to be the place to be. In most of the '70s, stocks were in pretty terrible shape.

Sprague started his professional career in 1978 at Oppenheimer Capital in New York working for Jim Smith, who had once worked for Bauer at American General. Sprague decided to accept a position with Oppenheimer because the company had no formal internal training program. As a result, Sprague was the beneficiary of training programs at Salomon Brothers, Merrill

Lynch, Morgan Stanley, Dillon Reed, and Goldman Sachs. "Basically, I had a two-year MBA process without actually having to get my masters," he recalled. "Part of my deal was that I would start at $12,000, which was less than what they were paying the secretary. When I showed up, they gave me a $500 raise because they didn't believe I would take the job.

"I went to the office Christmas party that year, and it was held on three floors. Oppenheimer had 1,500 employees at the time. The top floor was where the partners had their party. The officers were on the middle floor. The lower floor was for everybody else. The chairman of the company was Chuck Bruney, a great guy. The president was Larry Blum. But even though I was managing about a billion dollars at the age of 24, I realized then that the probability of becoming a partner at Oppenheimer was pretty slim.

"In the fall of 1979, the Federal Reserve had raised interest rates. The market thought it was a wonderful move and Chuck Bruney thought it was time to buy bonds. I went into an Investment Policy Committee meeting and, basically, was told to buy a low-grade bond and eight government agency securities for my accounts. I said I would love to do that, and I believe the thinking was right. But I had to buy single-A or better and I couldn't buy agencies. I could only buy U.S. Treasuries in my accounts. The chairman looked at me. I was by far the youngest of the 25 or so people in the room. Bruney was about 6-foot-9, a very imposing figure. He walked over, pulled out my chair and said, 'Thank you, Mr. Sprague, you may leave now.'

"I picked up my things and left. I may have been a little flippant in the way I said it, but I hadn't intended to be. I had the contracts in front of me and I just quoted what they said. But that wasn't what they wanted to hear."

Sprague went back to his trading desk to reflect on the situation. He thought he'd be fired on the spot if he were still in the office when the meeting ended, so he pulled his stuff together and walked across the street to a bar that seemed to be frequented mostly by brokers and traders. Little did Sprague know that his life was going to take another big turn the same day.

"Within minutes, Ted Bauer walked in," Sprague says. "I had met him once, through another friend, Brace Young, Sr., whose son was my college roommate. I started to introduce myself. He said, 'I know who you are. You're Abbott Sprague. You work with Jim Smith. You're a friend of Brace Young.'

"We sat and we talked for awhile and he said, 'Why don't you come with me uptown and join us for dinner? I'm meeting two of my partners, Bob Graham and Gary Crum, and Jack Painter, who manages our convertible portfolio. We can talk about what you are doing.'

"That's how I met Bob and Gary. Jim Smith really wanted to get back to Texas and I believe he had been talking to Ted. Jim and I had landed Tenneco as an account, and we were planning a trip to Houston. I had never been there. The dinner went well, and then we flew down and spent four days in Houston. AIM had just landed World Bank and Delta Airlines as separate accounts. So, they thought here was an opportunity to bring in two guys, Jim Smith and myself, who could bring in other accounts. They were focused primarily on fixed-income and high-yield, but we were more high-grade buyers.

"There was a birthday party that night at Bob Graham's house for one of the employees, and we were invited. During the night, I turned to Jim Smith and said, 'At this point, I can't really move down to this swamp.' It was January and the temperature was around 70 degrees. So I got back on a Braniff flight and halfway to New York I was looking out the window. It was a beautiful, clear night and we were flying over Philadelphia. You could probably see Pittsburgh in the distance. Then it hit me! This was something that I needed to do! I didn't negotiate any of my contract. Jim Smith did that for me. I actually moved down on my 25th birthday. I figured if I didn't like it after a year or two, I still had plenty of time."

Sprague moved in with the Bauers until he found a place of his own. Early on, he heard the most reassuring words a new employee can hear when Bauer told him, "You don't work for Jim Smith. You work for Ted Bauer."

"I've talked to a lot of people about this, and they all tell you how important it is to have a mentor," Sprague says. "And you couldn't have a better one. We looked at each other, and I said, 'I want your brain.' And Ted said, 'I want your age.' We built a very good relationship. Ted was best man at my wedding."

When Abbott Sprague talks about that special family feeling at AIM, he speaks with authority. He was the 16th employee hired by AIM, and has spent the better part of the last 20 years building the company's Institutional Marketing division. While many things have changed over time, the average age of AIM's employees has remained at or under 30. Those unfamiliar with the infrastructure needed for a successful mutual fund operation might figure this would be the average age of the staff at Disney World, not at a major financial institution. But age is just a number at AIM. And in the mutual fund industry, numbers are taken in stride.

*Part of AIM's fixed-income braintrust, left to right,
Karen Dunn Kelley, Bob Alley, and Stuart Coco, confer with
senior equity portfolio manager Jon Schoolar, front.*

"When I got here," says Sprague, "I didn't know what the company was doing in terms of revenues. There were a couple of times when Ted handed me my check that first year, where he said, 'Can you kind of hold onto this for a couple of days?' I don't know whether he was kidding or not, but certainly Ted will tell you that they kind of rocked along for a few years.

"We can talk about the funds we bought or acquired, but the measure of AIM's success was that we hired well. We wanted to be thin. We wanted to be lean. But AIM kept attracting strong people. So many have been here from the beginning, and a lot of others have now passed the 10-year mark. In this business, that speaks volumes. There is a sense here that people control their own destinies, that they're going to be heard, that they're not going to be shoved aside.

"This comes down from Ted. He didn't really want to have people who walked into their office, closed the door, and you never heard 'Boo' from them. Our employees are doers; they tend to be competitive. Ted encouraged us to go out and vent some of our frustrations, or aggressiveness, in healthy ways. Bob Graham played tag football for years. I played soccer. The tennis matches with Ted and Gary, Dave Barnard and the rest of us, went on for years. We'd try to beat the heck out of each other, just for fun. But as a group it brought us closer together."

One of Sprague's best hires at AIM proved to be someone he didn't originally interview. Karen Dunn Kelley had three separate interviews postponed at AIM when she first tried to get her foot in the door as a money market manager. She had worked at Drexel and Federated before marrying an oncologist who was on fellowship at Houston's M.D. Anderson Cancer Research Center. She planned to return to Pittsburgh once her husband completed his residency, but didn't want to place her career on hold. AIM had become one of the major money market managers in the country and was getting some of the first calls of any firm every morning.

"Once we hired Karen, we saw how capable she was and how she was going to grab hold," Bauer recalled. "She knew trading and compliance, she'd worked in back offices, and she could sell. You have to be able to make split-second decisions to be a good money manager; you don't want to haggle for a few basis points. And Karen is able to sell not by being fancy, but by telling you facts you'd never think you'd hear out of one person's mouth."

AIM had put together a research staff in the 1980s when the company was bringing its first money market funds. AIM's staff performed its own independent research on all money market credits before such steps were mandated by the SEC.

Kelley was hired as portfolio manager of AIM's three government funds on the money market side. There were three portfolios at the time."

"I wasn't home-grown," Kelley said. "I'd been on the sell side of the market. I had managed both short-term funds and long-term funds. Back then, AIM wasn't a very big firm. You hired somebody who had an expertise in an area, and if they could bring a couple of jacks-of-all-trades from different areas to the table, everybody pitched in and did whatever we could. Those were the days when the transfer agency, the custodian, portfolio management, and just about everyone else was sitting around the table.

"AIM is really the classic industry story in terms of how equity assets grew after October of '87. And AIM's success is directly related to the management culture. I remember once we were in a meeting with an outside firm on a very sticky subject. Things were getting a little heated, and Ted Bauer, being a great diplomat, knew the situation was getting tense. He got up, went over to the presenter, picked up a plate of cookies, and went around and hand-offered off this tray of cookies to everyone in the room. The whole exercise took him about three minutes and it changed the entire posture of the meeting. We accomplished what we had set out to do, although nobody really wanted to get it done."

Generally speaking, money market funds are considered relatively stable because of their short maturities and high quality. Most money market instruments are a short-term form of IOU issued by the U.S. government, U.S. corporations, and state and local governments. Most money market funds are required to invest at least 95 percent of assets in U.S. Treasury issues and privately issued securities carrying the highest credit rating by at least two of the five major credit rating agencies. Money market funds seek to maintain a net asset value of $1-per-share to preserve investment principal while generating dividend income. Only the interest rate goes up or down. Falling below the $1 NAV is called "breaking the buck" and can stain a fund company's reputation as a conservative asset manager. In order to satisfy client needs and expectations, AIM maintains a very conservative money market policy.

On the institutional side of the business, it is not uncommon for Kelley and her staff to take $100 million orders. And they have to be ready to respond to extreme scrutiny from institutional clients at any given time. When the bankruptcy of Orange County, California made headlines in 1994 as a result of a derivatives crisis, one of AIM's long-standing institutional customers called for an update on the funds.

"They called and said, 'We demand...' and they've never demanded anything before," Kelley said. "They were a $700 million account and were one of the five original investors in our STIC funds. We responded by going out there with a presentation for the funds that you could not believe. They had us on video conferencing all over the state to all of their senior people at the branches. The chairman of the bank sat there and said, 'We had to lose money for our customers in an oil crisis. We will not

Abbott Sprague asked Ted Bauer to serve as best man at his wedding.

do it in a derivatives crisis. We want to know what your policies are and where you are.'

"We told them that the money market side is a combination of safety, liquidity, and yield. That's why we didn't buy derivatives then. That's why we won't buy derivatives now. We went through every fund with them, every security we had in our portfolios. At the end they thanked us, and didn't take any money out. It's another example of the relationships AIM has built over the years."

Relationships are built from trust. Since money market funds aren't federally insured, companies must be confident that their investments are in good hands. Money market funds at several major fund companies attracted unwanted attention again in the summer of 1999. General American Life Insurance Company ran into financial problems, causing one major ratings agency to lower General American's credit rating. Concerned about the ability of General American to pay the $5 billion it had borrowed, more than 30 money market mutual funds demanded repayment. General American said it could pay back the funds, many of which were run by well-known firms. AIM, however, was not among the firms that invested in the funding agreements that sparked the controversy. Adhering to a conservative approach has enabled AIM to maintain a strong reputation among leading managers of institutional money market funds.

In 1989, AIM's Institutional Marketing division was expanded to compete in the increasingly competitive institutional fund arena. AIM registered Fund Management Company to act as distributor for AIM's institutional products. Because of the generic nature of its name, Fund Management Company became a more attractive partner for joint ventures with banks, since the name provided anonymity for bank customers who wish to promote their name and not the name of a mutual fund service vendor.

In the early 1990s, the institutional marketing environment was dominated by increasing merger-and-acquisition activity among banks. The rapidly changing institutional landscape prompted AIM to focus on two-long term goals – increase market penetration and achieve a level of superior customer service. In 1992, AIM began to establish niche markets such as credit unions, public funds, consultants, and insurance outlets.

Through persistency and perseverance, AIM's Institutional Marketing has become known as more than just a money market provider. Over the last six years it has tripled its staff, internalized its transfer agency function, and introduced an automated trading system – AIMLINK. Under Sprague's direction, AIM has expanded its institutional distribution opportunities and reinforced AIM's brand image through the coordinated efforts of its Financial Services Group, Consultant Services Group, and Product Marketing Group. National sales manager Mark Santero, regional sales managers Bill Hoppe, Bill Wendel, and Pat Bray, and institutional marketing manager Mike Rome were instrumental in growing AIM's institutional assets under management in 1999.

By the time Sprague had commemorated his 20th year of service in 2000, AIM's Institutional Division was handling more than 300 relationships with more than 10,000 accounts and more than $50 billion in money-market assets under management. Institutional Marketing fielded more than 100,000 calls from shareholders in 1999, partly as a result of its ability to create new products and better position itself as a dominant player in the sub-advisory business and growing cash sweep marketplace. Persistent volatility in equity markets had continued to underscore the importance AIM placed in safety, liquidity, and yield in the area of institutional money markets.

Chapter Twelve

GOING
DUTCH

In the late 1980s and early 1990s, AIM searched for a strong financial partner that would bring the company long-term stability no individual could provide. In addition to providing financial stability, the ideal partner AIM was seeking also would provide access to world markets and capital for expansion as well as instill confidence to employees and customers.

"After the market crash in 1987, when we weren't sure how prolonged it was going to be, some of our employees and members of the brokerage community probably were thinking to themselves, 'Is AIM going to be able to survive this?' Bob Graham recalled. "We felt we needed to do something to assure that we had the financial capability and would stand up for a long downturn. We had two very strict criteria. First, we wanted someone who would provide an infusion of capital for a minority interest. We also thought it would be good to have a European partner that could help us by providing access to important

The AIM Funds board of directors in the early 1990s. Seated, left to right, Lewis Pennock, Ted Bauer, and Owen Daly. Standing, left to right, Carl Frischling, John Kroeger, and Louis Sklar.

new markets overseas." AIM also was interested in relative autonomy in a corporate sense.

In 1988, AIM's senior management team enlisted the services of PaineWebber to seek a new partner, one which would replace French Peterson's position in the company and provide further capital through which AIM could accelerate its growth. Peterson had been one of the original investors in AIM. Within a few months, four parties had shown interest. Among them was Nationale-Nederlanden, N.V., a large Dutch insurance conglomerate that sent representatives to AIM for an initial visit in August 1988 and came away highly impressed. For a

Giant Dutch firm buying
22% stake in AIM group

By PAMELA YIP
Houston Chronicle

AIM Management Group said Wednesday it has reached an agreement in principle to sell about 22 percent of the company to Nationale-Nederlanden N.V., a giant Dutch insurance firm.

Executives of AIM, a Houston mutual fund company, said Nationale's participation will provide the deep pockets needed for AIM's expansion.

"We've got a banking source," said Charles T. Bauer, AIM chairman and chief executive. "While the outlook for the financial services industry is excel-

lent, we feel the basic nature of the business is changing toward broader product lines and greater capital intensity."

Nationale's 22 percent stake in AIM is being purchased through Nationale-Nederlanden Holdings Inc., the Dutch U.S. subsidiary. The parent company is based in The Netherlands.

The purchase price was disclosed.

The agreement also tionale to buy a new convertible preferred AIM. Bauer said a sion of the prefer about three years conditions are m

ntion of scooping in AIM.

Netherlands firm to buy 22 percent of AIM: company

By JANE BAIRD
OF THE HOUSTON POST STAFF

AIM Management Group Inc., a Houston-based mutual fund and money management firm, announced Wednesday that a large insurance company in the Netherlands plans to buy 22 percent of its stock.

Nationale-Nederlanden N.V. also plans to purchase a new series of convertible prefer-

Headlines from the *Houston Chronicle*
and *The Houston Post.*

*AIM received a Dutch treat when Nationale-Nederlanden
agreed to purchase 22 percent of the company in 1990.*

while, Nationale-Nederlanden officials weren't sure that AIM was a large enough company to pursue, but NN's senior U.S. representatives eventually sent a letter to AIM executives indicating an interest in negotiations.

Nationale-Nederlanden had only recently decided to enter the money management business in the U.S. when it first sent executives to visit AIM. Such a move was considered the next natural step for NN, which had just completed several acquisitions of insurance companies throughout North America and viewed the money management business as a highly profitable extension of its existing enterprise.

From AIM's perspective, NN was a potentially attractive partner for several reasons. As the largest insurance company in The Netherlands, it could provide a solid source of capital and help AIM gain valuable access to markets throughout Europe. Ted Bauer's blueprint for success for AIM in the 1990s included a vision of creating a platform for the global distribution of financial products, and a marriage of AIM and NN would be a viable first step. NN also had the insurance expertise and U.S. distribution necessary for AIM to test the variable annuity market for the first time, a longtime goal of Bauer's.

"What I believed we would get out of the experience was working with a rising star in the mutual fund business," recalled NN executive Tom Balachowski. "AIM is one of America's great success stories. We thought the people from AIM were of the highest integrity, and had the highest sense of values. Ted, Bob, and Gary understood insurance and the insurance mentality, which is very important to us, because there is a fundamental, cultural difference between insurance and other parts of the financial industry."

A two-year courtship developed between AIM and NN, with senior executives from AIM determined to retain majority interest as part of any deal. But some of AIM's original partners who were not part of management had become quite interested in selling their shares. The estate of French Peterson was interested in selling its 18 percent stake in AIM, and the London-based Schlesinger Group was seeking liquidity. Mandy Moross, for one, was interested in accelerating the search for a proper suitor that could buy a minority interest in AIM.

As part of the due diligence process, Bauer and Graham traveled to The Hague in April 1989 to continue negotiations with representatives of NN. On their way to The Netherlands, they stopped at Moross' house in the south of France. They arrived late one night after an all-day flight, had a late dinner with Moross, and retired to guest rooms in a state of near-exhaustion. "The next day,

I'm still sound asleep at noon and Mandy had become impatient to talk business," Graham recalled. " He threw open the drapes in my room to let the sun in and said, 'Bob, I'm sure you don't want to sleep this late! It's time to get up!'

"Mandy had this beautiful house in St. Jean Cap-Ferrat overlooking the bay there. It's an absolutely spectacular place. He wanted to know what we were going to talk about with NN. We went on to meet the fellow there who was in charge of their North American operations at the time, a guy named Otto Hattink, who is a brilliant person, a most impressive guy. He understood immediately what we were trying to do. A few months later, he called Ted and told him they were interested, but needed a way to acquire control."

But that's not the kind of deal that interested AIM. Negotiations continued for several more months before a compromise was reached in May 1990. NN agreed to purchase a 20 percent interest in AIM for approximately $4.5 million in a move that bought out the shares held by French Peterson's estate. NN also paid $5 million for preferred stock that gave the company the option to gain a controlling interest in AIM in three years. Should NN decide to exercise its option in 1993, it would be able to buy out Moross and his fellow shareholders and end up with a 60 percent controlling interest in one of America's most promising mutual fund companies.

"We had a very nice arrangement for our shares with them in which we had a formula price that hopefully would continue to go up and they couldn't call our stock; we could only put it to them," Bauer said. "It was a one-way deal. We felt we had done about the best we could in a situation where you had to give up control."

During the next three years, AIM continued to make headlines in the U.S. mutual fund industry. Assets under management increased 30 percent to $16 billion in 1991. The purchase of 14 funds from CIGNA helped produce similar double-digit increases in assets in each of the next two years as a result of strong fund performance combined with aggressive retail marketing and distribution. AIM's earnings surged from $4.2 million in 1990 to $23.1 million in 1992. Times were good. And although the synergies AIM hoped would develop overseas as a result of NN's minority stake never quite materialized, senior management fully expected NN to exercise its option in 1993.

"They sent a team of five people down here in December 1992," Graham said. "They spent several days with us trying to figure what we were all about. We thought that meeting went fairly well. They had one gentleman down here who understood our business better than the others because he had done a lot of trading in emerging country debts. He understood speculative trading and securities and was a trader at heart and empathized with our business more than some of the insurance-company types. He was very enthusiastic about having his company exercise the option."

Graham was on business in Tucson and missed the next team of Dutch executives which came on a due diligence mission to AIM in February 1993, three months before the option was to expire. Only a few weeks later, Bauer received a fax from NN executives saying the company had, indeed, decided to exercise its option.

"I went off to a mutual funds conference in Palm Springs in March with my wife Annie thinking, 'This is going to be great,'" Graham said. "Why? Nationale-Nederlanden had agreed to the concept that there had to be some sort of equity participation. They had said from the beginning that they believed very strongly in local autonomy, that they did not try to micro-manage all of their units. We had talked to some of their CEOs and presidents of some of their subsidiaries who confirmed this. They said they didn't bother you as long as you lived up to your plan, which is what we wanted."

Only 10 days after the original fax was received saying NN had decided to renew its option, and with Graham having just left for California, Bauer received one of the shortest, yet most important business phone calls in AIM's history. Aad Jacobs of NN called Bauer to inform AIM of a change of heart. The company had decided not to exercise its option. "Well, you've made a big mistake," Bauer said. "But so be it. And please send me a follow-up letter," he added, before ending the conversation.

Hours later, Graham returned to his Palm Springs hotel room and received an urgent message to call Bauer.

"Are you sitting down?" Bauer asked.

"Yes," Graham replied, unaware of the news about to be delivered.

"They've changed their mind. They're not going to exercise their option."

Graham was speechless. The shocking message Bauer communicated meant everything AIM's co-founders had thrown their heart and soul into building over the last 17 years had fallen into disarray. Several long-term, non-management shareholders had been counting on a takeover by NN to sell their shares. AIM was faced with the arduous task of having to recapitalize the company or find a new partner that may or may not share the same vision of AIM's founders. "Even though we had been growing rapidly, we still weren't at the size where anyone considered us a serious competitor in the fund industry," Graham said. "The news was a huge disappointment to me."

NN's decision not to take advantage of its investment ownership option was based, in part, on the fact that the formula price held by members of AIM's management team had increased from $15 to $108 per share. NN was faced with a hefty $100 million price tag if it wanted to gain majority control. It also would have to deal with the management share puts at a future date. At the time, experts valued AIM at approximately $300 million, meaning NN would have to pay $240 million for the 80 percent of AIM it didn't own.

Graham immediately began trying to think of alternatives AIM could pursue while he was still in attendance at an Investment Company Institute conference that included many of the movers and shakers in the mutual fund industry. "I saw Roberto de Guardiola the next day at the conference and told him that NN had changed its mind. He mentioned TA Associates as a firm that might be interested in doing something. Mandy had pretty much anticipated being taken out by NN at that stage and we felt it was important to go ahead and try to get liquidity for him. And we didn't see any reason to keep NN in, even though they said they would be perfectly happy to stay as a minority shareholder. We weren't interested in having a big conglomerate come in and buy them out."

In addition to its equity position, NN had also loaned money to the company. In order to raise the money required for this buyout and to pay off the NN loan and other outstanding loans from banks, AIM structured a deal with Citibank. As lead bank of a syndicate of eight

Bob Graham, left, had frequent meetings with chief financial officer
Dawn Hawley and chief legal counsel Bill Kleh during
AIM's recapitalization in 1993.

or nine banks, Citibank agreed to lend AIM $180 million, of which $170 million was to go towards the buyout and $10 million was for working capital. However, the banks wanted the company to have equity held by an entity other than management personnel. Talks were held with a number of leverage buyout firms, but they all wanted to obtain a majority position in the company which was unacceptable to management.

Only TA Associates was willing to be strictly an investor. "I think Andy McLane and his partners at TA Associates were sold on AIM's management," de Guardiola recalled. "They decided that in a money management company, people are far more important than votes."

A recapitalization was designed in which management stockholders sold to affiliates of TA Associates about 32 percent of its holdings held prior to the recap for $35 million at $33.75 per share. After the recap, which included the buyout of most of the non-management shareholders, over 68 percent of the company's stock was owned by management personnel.

The Citibank loan was in four tranches with maturities ranging from three to seven years and bore a viable rate of interest. The company's management was concerned that AIM would be exposed to greater interest expense in the event of rising interest rates. Consequently, the company arranged for the sale of $110 million of 9 percent Senior Secured Notes, due in the year 2003, through an underwriting syndicate led by Merrill Lynch, the proceeds of which were used to reduce the company's bank loans.

"It ended up being a very complicated process," Graham said. "We felt the end result was going to be a highly leveraged company and we didn't want to get in a very leveraged situation without taking some money out ourselves. Once we got the $170 million bank financing in place, we didn't want to be dependent on interest rates. Then we got into a big argument as to whether we needed a shareholder vote. We originally took the position that nobody had control of AIM prior to the recapitalization and nobody had control after the recap, so there was no change in control. However, Merrill Lynch, which was going to be the underwriter of the bonds, told us their legal counsel was not comfortable with that. They wanted to have a shareholder meeting so there would be no doubt." Mandy Moross stood in the middle because of the impasse and was instrumental in helping the sides reach a final agreement.

Things became so hectic in the summer of '93 that Graham and his family were joined on their annual trip to a Montana dude ranch by two lawyers and two investment bankers. "The problem was, there was only one phone at the dude ranch," Graham said. "I remember going with my family on an all-day horseback trip to Yellowstone Park. When I got back at 11 o'clock that night, I had a message to call Dawn Hawley at some hotel. They needed a decision on something that was holding up the bank closing.

"We ended up having to put the money in escrow so we couldn't purchase the stock until there had been a shareholder meeting. And we couldn't close the bond deal until the shareholder meeting. We did the bank financing in June 1993, and that brought the money in. We did the road show for the bonds in September and October and then everything came out of escrow. Ultimately, we ended up with a situation where management controlled about 70 percent of the company and TA Associates owned approximately 30 percent. They took Class B shares so they stayed under 25 percent voting control, but we had $170 million in debt.

The company's net worth had dropped from $120 million to $40 million. We had an ugly-looking balance sheet and it was a very difficult process, but we knew what the end result would be – that management was going to be firmly in control of this company and we would be in control of our own destiny."

Chapter Thirteen

FUNDS®

WHEAT IN
THE BARN

Although the business synergies that AIM hoped
would develop during its three-year affiliation with
Nationale-Nederlanden never fully materialized, the relationship did produce one landmark accomplishment. Part
of the original deal included a $10 million loan from NN,
which AIM used to acquire the CIGNA Funds in June
1992. The acquisition capped a series of negotiations that
stretched out over three years and provided AIM with the
slingshot effect it needed to move into the ranks of the
nation's 10 largest mutual fund companies.

AIM and CIGNA were first brought to the negotiating table by Roberto de Guardiola, a long-time friend of
Gary Crum's and the most important matchmaker in
AIM's history. De Guardiola was a bond trader at Kidder
Peabody when he first met Crum in the 1970s. "Roberto
was from a fairly prominent family in Havana, Cuba, that
emigrated to the United States and started again from

scratch in Palm Beach, Florida," Crum said. "He went on to get a first-class education. He was in charge of the corporate bond department at PaineWebber for a while. He was hired away by Kleinwort back when everybody was trying to go global in the '80s. As I recall, they gave him a big raise and a two-year, no-cut contract. But then the bond market took a major dive and Roberto found himself out of work. He became a consultant and made it his business to know all the top guns on Wall Street."

De Guardiola called Crum one day when he read that AIM had failed to purchase a fund managed out of California. "He knew the people at CIGNA because he used to cover corporate bonds," Crum said. "He introduced us to them in the summer of 1990, but nothing came of it and things didn't resurface for another year."

AIM was interested in the CIGNA funds because it felt it needed to acquire a wide range of equity and fixed-income products to broaden its retail product line. But at the time, CIGNA was more interested in coping with the bear market of 1990 than selling its mutual fund operation. One year later, de Guardiola called Bob Graham to say he had a friend who was working with him on trying to sell some funds and wanted to know if AIM would talk to him about the possibilities.

Graham met de Guardiola in the Parkway Hotel in New York and was told of a company that had become interested in selling its mutual fund business. "Roberto gave us some parameters and we told him we were interested," Graham said. "He never mentioned the name of the company, but when we returned to Houston we quickly figured out the company was CIGNA."

De Guardiola had gone to Larry English, the head of the fund group of CIGNA at the time, and convinced him

Roberto de Guardiola: The mutual fund industry's version of
Monte Hall, and the most famous matchmaker in AIM history.

that CIGNA should sell its funds. "Roberto was unique," English said. "Unlike a lot of investment bankers who waited for the clients to come to them to look for a buyer, Roberto was going out and talking to various owners of mutual funds and trying to convince them to sell."

CIGNA had several funds with above-average performance records, but lacked the necessary distribution to grow the mutual fund business. AIM, meanwhile, was putting together a standout retail distribution operation under the direction of Mike Cemo, but needed the kind of mutual fund products CIGNA had to offer.

De Guardiola is a firm believer that it's easier to structure a deal by skipping formalities and linking parties who can combine for win-win situations. "When I'm talking to a potential seller, what I'm really saying to them is, 'Look. I know such-and-such is calling on you and I know they're telling you to let them represent you," de Guardiola says. "They can write a nice book and send out 100 copies and out of the 100 firms contacted, 10 will submit bids. Out of those 10, three will be good, and you can meet with them and you can put them all in competition. That's the pitch that my investment banking friends will make to a potential seller. But I'm telling you to forget all that. Don't bother writing a book. Don't do any of that stuff. Just sit down with my good friend Ted Bauer and in an hour, you can probably come to a deal."

With de Guardiola serving as the go-between, representatives from AIM and CIGNA met in Hartford, Connecticut, to try to reach an agreement. "We tried to convince CIGNA they should sell to us because we could open up their distribution," Cemo said. "In this industry, you get to a point where the distribution you have has a limit. And if you don't sell as much as 15 percent of your net assets – which is the normal redemption rate – you're just spinning your wheels."

English, however, said he couldn't sell the CIGNA funds as part of negotiations that included only one bidder. Pioneer then entered the picture as a possible suitor, but AIM was able to put together a more attractive package. "In effect, CIGNA could make up its mind who they wanted to sell the business to based on personality issues and who they thought the best fit was with," de Guardiola recalled. "The financial part of these transactions is always the easiest part. We can always, in a very short period of time – hours, if not minutes – come up with a price that is within 90-95 percent of the final bid."

Many of the nine fixed-income and five equity funds AIM purchased have since become household names,

AIM Management to absorb mutual funds of giant insurer CIGNA

By PAMELA YIP
Houston Chronicle

Aim Management Group has agreed to take over as manager and investment adviser for 14 mutual funds run by the Cigna Cos., the companies announced Friday.

The move follows Aim's past strategy of growing by assuming management of already established funds, analysts said.

Both companies declined to release terms of the transaction.

Aim and Cigna said the alliance would enable each to offer more investment options to investors and take advantage of the giant insurer's sales force.

This deal will also make it possible for Cigna and Aim to joint

vestment opti... variable annu... The 14 fu... assets inves... cash. They... The funds... Aim's H... investm... Group... that... man... insu...

Under the AIM umbrella

Aim Management Group of Houston has agreed to take over management of 14 mutual funds now managed by Cigna. If the deal goes through, it would raise Aim's total assets under management to $19.7 billion and increase the number of Aim funds available to individual investors from 10 to 24.

Fund	Assets
Cigna Cash Fund	
Cigna Money Market Fund	
Cigna Tax-Exempt Fund	$88 million
Cigna Tax-Exempt Cash Fund of Conn.	$110 million
Cigna Government Securities Fund	$45 million
Cigna Municipal	$21 million
Cigna Tax-Exempt Bond of Conn.	$110 million
Cigna High Yield Fund	$267 million
Cigna Income Fund	$30 million
Cigna Utilities Fund	$281 million
Cigna Value Fund	$220 million
Cigna Growth Fund	$91 million
Cigna Aggressive Growth	$169 million
Cigna International Growth	$177 million
	$18 million
	$7 million

Source: Aim Management Group

Chronicle

Headlines from the *Houston Chronicle*.

The purchase of 14 funds from insurer CIGNA ensured AIM's success in the early 1990s.

most notably AIM Value Fund, AIM Aggressive Growth Fund, and AIM High Yield Fund. Other funds which came over from CIGNA included AIM Income Fund, AIM Global Utilities Fund, AIM Tax-Free Bond Fund of Connecticut, AIM Select Growth Fund, an international equity fund, and AIM Municipal Bond Fund. Total assets of the 14 funds was approximately $1.6 billion, for which AIM paid approximately $35 million. At the time, Bauer said AIM's acquisition of the CIGNA funds was "like putting wheat in the barn."

"Ted may pay at the top end, but he ends up acquiring funds that aren't being sold," said Bill Kleh, who served as AIM's chief legal counsel from 1986-1998. "He realizes that current owners can't sell them, for whatever reason, and capitalizes on the fact he can." Indeed, in less than eight years, the assets in the funds AIM purchased from CIGNA had increased to more than $40 billion.

"The CIGNA deal was interesting because there was a follow-on payment structured into the deal," Kleh added. "The theory was that CIGNA would help sell the funds through its insurance sales force if we would give them an incentive. So we had a follow-on payment that depended on the asset growth of the funds we acquired from them. We never thought in our wildest imagination that it would really require us to pay any more money. But we did. We had to write them a huge check because we built them into a powerhouse."

The addition of the CIGNA funds prompted quick growth in several areas throughout the company. Portfolio managers had to be added, a new distribution channel was opened, and phone representatives had to be hired and trained. Members of AIM's equity department, such as Bob Kippes and Joel Dobberpuhl, went to visit Harry Hutzler in New York for two-week periods as part of their training to become portfolio managers.

Jon Schoolar was named chief equity officer and continued to serve as lead manager on AIM Weingarten Fund and AIM Constellation Fund. Bob Alley was hired as chief fixed-income officer from Waddell & Reed in Kansas City after Crum studied a Lipper list of the nation's top-performing income funds. Alley had put together a sterling record with the Waddell & Reed Income Fund. "When we bought the CIGNA funds, we also had to bring in a broader range of investment analyst," said Stuart Coco, AIM's director of fixed-income research. "As we've added assets in the areas, we've added personnel, each more specialized than before."

Retail marketing continued its expansion under Cemo with the addition of a distribution channel to service independent insurance agents and financial planners. Gordon Sprague, whose previous business endeavors included teaching Dale Carnegie classes and working for former Kansas City Royals owner Avron Fogelman, was brought in as national sales manager of the IIDD channel and its three wholesalers and four marketing specialists.

"We call on the financial planner, the insurance agent, the private contractor, or the NASD firm person who is not connected with an NYSE firm," Sprague says. "Their retention of assets tends to be much higher than the rate of other channels. About 80 percent of assets sold by the financial planner or the independent and insurance side is with us 12 months later. Most commonly, they don't care what the market did yesterday or what it's going to do tomorrow. If they learn a competitor's story and they've had reasonably good service over the years, they will keep selling that product from that company because they've never embarrassed them. What drives them is not making the sale of the product, it's finding the client who has the need and satisfying that with whatever product they choose.

"We call on single people all day long because most planners are one- or two-person shops. Our wholesalers probably will have to take an entire month to see as many people as a wirehouse wholesaler can see in one day. In terms of our division and the audience we call on, we want strong relationships.

"You ask what the key ingredient is to be a wholesaler and I'll say just show me anybody who has a burning desire to be successful. It doesn't matter what their background is. If they know what a wholesaler does and they want to commit themselves to that life and have an unfailing ability to succeed, they will make it. They just have to want it badly enough. It's a very lonely world. It's very difficult for someone young who's courting somebody to lead the life a hard-working wholesaler does. It's extremely difficult for someone with young children. It's actually easier for someone who's older, who is past that point in his or her life.

"A well-organized wholesaler would have a breakfast meeting scheduled early in the morning. He then would probably stop in to see one or two people in the morning, whether by invitation or appointment. Then there would be a lot of phone calls and e-mails to return before a lunch meeting. Hopefully, the afternoon would repeat itself with two or three more visits. I've been told that the average life of a wholesaler is less than that of an NFL player, which is three years."

Sprague left the IIDD channel in early 2000 to join AIM's parent company AMVESCAP as a senior partner in the development of retail strategies for AMVESCAP's Canadian and Asian affiliates. Sprague was succeeded by longtime AIM wholesaler Jim Stueve.

Having a wider variety of products to sell also prompted AIM to create a Financial Institutions Division in 1993. The FID channel was designed to enable AIM to increase its penetration of bank retail dealers, an area the company believed would embrace the concept of dual pricing. "At the time, AIM was viewed as a niche player promoting equities," said Mike Vessels, hired from Putnam in 1993 to serve as FID national sales manager. "When I joined AIM, the company was ranked No. 12 in terms of sales through the bank channel. The following year, we came up to No. 5."

AIM's FID and IIDD channels were taking root at about the same time AIM Weingarten Fund began to encounter short-term performance challenges. At the end of 1991, the industry's top growth funds spiked. Bauer, believing that 1992 might turn out to be a repeat of the bear market of 1973-74, tried to persuade the funds' managers to change emphasis from relying solely on earnings growth. But it took over a year to convince them. And by then, it was too late.

The "Nifty Fifty" was a group of stocks whose collapse ultimately fueled the 1973-74 bear market. These were companies like Avon and Xerox that had good management and excellent growth prospects. According to the conventional wisdom, the only decision an investor had to make with these stocks was to buy them. These stocks, which at one time sold at price to earnings ratios of 80 or more, supposedly would grow forever, so you never had the make the decision to sell.

But many investors soon decided otherwise. Although the Nifty Fifty may have been a list of 50 good stocks, they were overpriced. After the Arab oil embargo and the 1973-74 recession, many investors made another decision and sold the stocks. The Nifty Fifty soon collapsed. The rest of the market wasn't spared, either, with the Dow losing 45 percent before it bottomed at 577 points in 1974.

Although AIM Weingarten Fund enjoyed record sales, fund performance was flat in '92 and '93. Wall Street temporarily had abandoned reliance on earnings momentum in favor of a more value-oriented investment approach.

Gordon Sprague helped AIM continue to grow its asset base through
sales to financial planners and independent broker/dealers.

Some of the stocks in AIM Weingarten Fund's portfolio
continued to have earnings growth, but the multiples the
market had placed on their earnings had become so enormous that their earnings trends could not support the
price levels the stocks had attained. Weingarten, true to
Hutzler's investment strategy, refused to sell these stocks
which had not broken their upward earnings trends and
the fund suffered as such stocks fell out of favor.

One year after the addition of the CIGNA funds, AIM also made an important move to become more competitive in the retail marketplace with the introduction of Class B shares on selected funds. Until then, AIM funds had only been sold with a front-end sales charge, or Class A shares. But the concept of Class B shares had become increasingly popular among financial advisors.

Under this alternative method, instead of paying a sales charge at the time of purchase, 100 percent of the purchase price was invested in Class B fund shares. The investor agreed to have a sales charge deducted from the proceeds if a redemption were made within seven years from the date of purchase. The amount of this contingent deferred sales charge deducted from the redemption was reduced each year until nothing was deducted from redemptions made after approximately seven years. The dealer was paid a commission at the time of sale, usually at the reduced rate of 4 percent, a fee which was paid by the fund distributor.

In addition to agreeing to a contingent deferred sales charge, the investor agreed to have a small amount, typically 75 basis points, deducted from the value of his or her fund shares annually to reimburse the fund distributor for advancing the dealer commission at the time of purchase. This new method gave the investor the choice of paying a sales charge in a lump sum up-front or choosing a pay-as-you-go plan over a six- or seven-year period.

This method of sales was pioneered by stock exchange member firms in selling their own funds. Since, typically, a selling dealer firm paid its salesmen about 50 percent of the commission, such member firms only had to finance the up-front commission at a 2 percent rate, the amount it paid its own salesmen. Since it was the only dealer selling shares of its sponsored funds, it could dispense with paying itself the 2 percent retained by the selling dealer.

AIM, however, sold its funds through independent dealers and therefore would have to finance the entire 4 percent paid to the dealer up-front. This required a payment of $40 million for each $500 million dollars of fund sales, the primary reason independent fund distributors such as AIM were not among the first mutual fund firms offering this new method of distribution. Nevertheless, brokers were clamoring to offer their clients this alternative method of purchase and AIM found it necessary to fall in line.

The company's financing of Class B shares was provided as part of the Citibank credit facility that originally had been set up to provide money for AIM's recapitalization in 1993 and had been reduced through the Merrill Lynch underwritten note offering. AIM began an active distribution of Class B shares on selected funds in September 1993 and had exhausted loans of over $235 million by the spring of 1996.

As another side benefit of its business dealings with CIGNA, AIM also wanted to enter the growing variable annuity business and considered CIGNA a capable partner. It was viewed as a potential win-win situation in that CIGNA could derive revenue from the variable annuity management fees while AIM kept the fund management fees. "Larry English thought getting together on a variable annuity product was a great idea, but we had to get an exemption from Nationale-Nederlanden in order to do so," Bauer said. "Nationale-Nederlanden decided they didn't want to be in the variable annuity business, so we

The purchase of the CIGNA funds created a need for additional portfolio management at AIM. Front row, Gary Crum, Harry Hutzler, and Dale Griffin. Back row, Bob Kippes, Dave Barnard, Joel Dobberpuhl, and Craig Smith. Kippes was placed on AIM Aggressive Growth Fund and Dobberpuhl on AIM Value Fund, a pair of CIGNA acquisitions, in 1992.

were able to jointly design seven variable annuity accounts with CIGNA which essentially cloned existing AIM funds."

The AIM/CIGNA Heritage Variable Annuity represented AIM's first step in the variable annuity business. Bauer had first suggested the idea to CIGNA during AIM's purchase of the CIGNA funds in 1992. In 1995, AIM fortified its position in the market as the result of a phone call from Lou Lower of Allstate Life Insurance Company. Lower was fascinated by AIM's rapid growth and suggested the two companies combine on another variable annuity product. Since then, AIM has developed 17 variable annuity funds, another example of the company's explosive growth.

Chapter Fourteen

EXPECT
EXCELLENCE

Making quality products available through strong distribution channels is only part of what it takes to grow business in the mutual fund industry. Fund performance may make the initial sale possible. But in the long run, service is paramount. Many companies have found that outgrowing their service facilities greatly damaged their sales efforts, and AIM realized it needed to take bold steps in the early 1990s to keep from being victimized by its own success.

"You pull the customer in because the broker thinks you have good funds," Ted Bauer says. "But they stay there because you are giving good service. If I want to change my address, put in new money, extract money, whatever the case, I need to be able to reach people who can help me. If a fund company doesn't have that, it has absolutely nothing."

Jack Caldwell emphasized the concept of outstanding client service
to support AIM's superior investment performance
and excellent marketing and distribution.

Mutual fund shareholder servicing performs the role
of a record keeper of shareholder accounts as well as a
transaction processor, tasks normally performed by a
transfer agent. In addition, good servicing requires a well-
trained telephone answering staff to respond to shareholder and broker inquiries. These functions can be performed internally or be farmed out to an outside vendor.
Until 1991, AIM's transfer agent was an outside entity,
and the processing of transactions and responding to
telephone inquiries were divided between AIM and its
transfer agent.

The addition of the Weingarten, Constellation, and
Charter Funds to AIM's product line had greatly increased
the need for quality customer service. AIM began search-
ing for an experienced industry executive who could
come in and address a challenging situation. But not even

AIM's Chairman's Council at work assisting top-producing
financial advisors with client service: Foreground, Allyson Dubose.
From left to right, Cher Murphy, Lea Thurman, Jenny Paulk,
Ty Spieker, and Matt Read.

Jack Caldwell knew what he was getting into when he left the Templeton Funds in St. Petersburg, Florida, and accepted the role as the head of AIM's internal transfer agent in 1991.

"I was in charge of the transfer agency there, was very happy, and had no plans of leaving," Caldwell said. "But I decided to look into the opportunity when they called me. I met with Bob Graham and Gary Crum the night I arrived and went into the AIM office the next day. That's when I met Ted Bauer and Mike Cemo and a few other people and came away with a good feeling about the company. The company was small, but it seemed real exciting and they were growing very fast at the time."

Caldwell had started his career with State Street Bank in Boston and then went to Colonial Funds, where he was involved with wholesaling and compliance operations. He went back into the operations side of the industry because the type of work appealed to him. "It never gets boring," Caldwell says. "You have a lot of contact with people, and that's what I like."

One of the first problems Caldwell was asked to solve involved $20 million in receivables AIM had from late payments from dealers on trades placed more than seven days earlier. Industry regulations require dealers to pay for fund share orders within seven days. With only 42 employees in client services, AIM simply did not have the staff to follow up on these delinquent orders. Worse yet, hundreds of phone calls to AIM every afternoon were going unanswered. Caldwell was trying to sort through the mess during his second day on the job when Cemo paid a visit.

"Do you realize they shut down the phones here every day at 2 o'clock, even on April 15?" Cemo said.

"What do you mean?" Caldwell replied.

"I mean they just don't take any calls after 2 o'clock and I have dealers complaining because they can't get through in the afternoon! They're too busy processing the paper, so they shut off the phones!"

Caldwell immediately rearranged the department's work processes and 25 additional people were hired. There was no space for them, so they were temporarily housed in the company's small auditorium. "AIM's technology and telecommunications groups did an outstanding job in just two days to set up the necessary equipment and phones in the auditorium 'war room' and temps were seated in place Monday morning to help them handle the volume," said Judy Creel.

Training was difficult as the new hires represented a 60 percent increase in personnel. "Since the new employees didn't have any training, we only showed them one or two items they could do per transaction," Caldwell recalls. "Then we'd have our senior people walking around, explaining how to do it. It was chaotic, but we had to get through it, and we did. I contacted some industry sources and I was able to get probably the best trainer in the industry in Lois Murphy.

"In the past 10 years, operations has become a very important factor in the industry because you can get good performance from a number of fund groups that are sold by broker/dealers and you can get very good sales support. But if you don't have the service, then the dealers can go someplace else and get the good performance *and* good sales support. The last thing a broker wants to have is a problem with an account because to them, every sale is a referral and if the transfer agent screws up the transaction, it's embarrassing for the dealer to go back to the client and ask for more referrals. He might even lose the client altogether.

"Little things can aggravate a client. When you're making an investment, sometimes it's a good part of your overall assets and you can lose confidence in companies if they don't spell your name right or get something corrected in a prompt, efficient manner."

Members of the AIM Funds' Board of Directors also place a high priority on providing quality service for clients. "The directors of the funds represent the shareholders," says fund director Owen Daly. "It's a little bit different than any other business because the directors of regular business corporations are pretty much brought on by management. Any time the independent trustees of a mutual fund company either individually or collectively

Hundreds of AIM client service representatives field thousands of calls from financial advisors and fund shareholders each business day.

make a point, it is well-listened to by the management company because they recognize it's coming from the trustees who represent the shareholders.

"It's management's primary concern to keep the shareholders happy, and you have to provide quality service. Consider all the glitches that are possible in the thousands of telephone calls, transactions and statements. You have to provide service to the brokers that do so much of the business and you have to keep your directors and trustees informed 100 percent about what you, meaning company management, are attempting to do for the benefit of the various funds. I think the main challenge is just to continually do what you're doing better because quality is the answer for survival."

Shortly after his arrival, Caldwell established a long-term goal of having AIM take over the transfer agency function of its retail funds from its outside vendor – The

Shareholder Services Group. "I felt that if we were to continue to grow and meet the objectives that Ted Bauer and Mike Cemo had, we had to be our own transfer agent," he said. "You can't depend on someone else servicing your customers."

In a relatively short time, the internal servicing capability had improved to the point AIM was able to take over most of the customer service operation by May 1994. Six months later, AIM completed the successful internalization of its transfer agency, and AIM Fund Services (AFS) was handling everything from telephone calls to transaction processing.

"The benefit in doing that was making it more timely," Caldwell says. "It's more accurate than it would be with a third-party processor because they're doing it with other clients, so they can get bogged down by other pressures. Most major mutual fund companies have their own in-house transfer agent now."

At the same time AIM was internalizing its transfer agency functions, the company was making necessary improvements in technology to offer quality customer service. A micrographics system was added which allowed every incoming item to be microfilmed and assigned a tracking number as an audit trail. This simple step enabled AIM to reduce research time from an average of 10 business days to one business day.

The addition of an Interactive Voice Response (IVR) system also was launched in 1994, an enhancement that enabled AIM fund shareholders and dealers to access account information 24 hours a day, seven days a week, using a touch-tone telephone. The IVR system, known as the AIM Investor Line, alleviated the burden placed on

*A meeting of the minds in AIM Fund Services. Left to right,
former training director Lois Murphy, retirement plans director Mary
Corcoran, Summit Plans manager Lisa Howie, correspondence director
Kim McAuliffe, Nina Maceda, client service manager Laura Slowensky,
and manager of brokerage operations and commissions Ira Cohen.*

AIM's growing client services staff by handling 25 percent of incoming calls.

"In January, our hold time might be more than 20 seconds because shareholders call with questions after they
receive their IRS Form 1099s in the mail," Caldwell says.
"But we try to keep our hold time down to five seconds or
less, and we try to keep our abandon rate to less than 3
percent. Right now, each of our reps is handling about
80-85 calls a day, but that can increase to about 140 in
January. The average call lasts about 2½ minutes."

AFS handled more than 1.2 million phone calls in
1995, the first full year it served as transfer agent for
AIM's retail funds. The number of AIM shareholder
accounts more than doubled between 1993 and 1995,
prompting the company to select Austin as a site for a

second facility that could service and process transfer agent activity. The close proximity to Houston was an important factor in selecting Austin because of business recovery considerations and the importance of having transfer agent functions available to shareholders and dealers whenever markets are open.

Caldwell joined Creel, Bob Graham and Gary Crum, among AIM executives present for a ribbon-cutting ceremony in April 1996 that commemorated AIM's new presence on two floors of the Temple-Inland Building at 301 Congress in Austin. The site officially opened on July 2, 1996, and is primarily responsible for servicing brokers in the Independence and Insurance Dealer Division channel in retail marketing.

AIM's steady growth in the late 1990s continued to place additional emphasis on the need for quality customer service. To meet these challenges, AIM enlisted an outside consultant in 1997 to help AFS achieve its goal of becoming a premier service provider. An AFS vision of quality, entitled Expect Excellence, was formulated and six desirable behavior attributes were identified and defined, giving form to the AFS ideas of quality. The six attributes – accuracy, attitude, ease of doing business, knowledge, responsiveness, and timeliness – are now used in all measurements of department and staff performance.

To complement AIM's internal Expect Excellence programs, AFS engages two external sources to measure quality – DALBAR, Inc. and National Quality Review. Monthly and quarterly, these firms report on AIM's progress and identify specific areas that may require improvement or change. AFS also conducts surveys with

Bob Graham, left and Gary Crum officially open AIM's new Austin facility in 1996. Joining Graham and Crum in the ceremony are Linda Warriner and Jack Caldwell of AIM Fund Services.

shareholders and dealers designed around the six key attributes to determine how service is perceived.

In 2000, AFS received the DALBAR Mutual Fund Service Award, which recognizes achievement of the highest tier of service to shareholders. The award was granted to only nine firms chosen from among 60 fund groups. DALBAR identified the winning firms through its Performance Evaluation of Mutual Fund Service Program. Within the program, DALBAR played the role of the investor and graded each firm on the customer service it received. The program examines mutual fund shareholder service with both qualitative and quantitative measures, such as timeliness of processing and the competence of telephone representatives. DALBAR looks at each firm's performance over an entire year of testing.

*Bob Graham, right, talks to a shareholder during the second reopening
of AIM Aggressive Growth Fund. Left to right, Ira Cohen,
Tony Green, and Cecilia Edwards of AFS.*

AFS focuses on continuous improvement through
advancements in technology and staff training. "With
each congressional session's changes to the law and the
continuing needs for sales and marketing innovations, the
transfer agency business has become very complex,"
Caldwell says. "We must continue to develop new training programs to refresh the old in order to provide staff
with the tools and knowledge to service our customers."

The best example of the need for staff training
occurred in 1998, when AIM added 25 former GT Global
funds to its retail lineup. Staff training totaled more than
75,000 hours involving more than 2,000 participants
because multiple training classes were required as part of
the conversion of the former GT Global shareholder

accounts to AFS's transfer-agent system. Over Labor Day weekend alone, more than 640,000 open accounts and 250,000 closed accounts with 7.3 million history records were successfully converted.

By early 2000, Caldwell's staff had grown to more than 700, and AFS was servicing approximately 5 million shareholder accounts. An additional 1.6 million AIM fund shareholder accounts were handled by other service providers. More than 2 million incoming calls were handled by AFS in 1999, and an additional 1.2 million calls were handled by the IVR system AIMLINE. The Account Balance page of AIM's Web site, www.aimfunds.com, also had become a popular method of communication for shareholders and financial advisors looking for updated information 24 hours a day, seven days a week. The site frequently has been cited as one of the best among mutual fund companies for financial professionals and institutional investors.

"I'm very satisfied with where the operation is going, but you can't rest on your laurels," says Caldwell, who is retiring in 2000 and will be succeeded by Tony Green. "We always have to look for ways to improve our service and be more competitive so the dealers will use our products more."

Chapter Fifteen

AIM
FUNDS.

RAGING
BULLS

Financial markets in 1994 were dominated by the action of the Federal Reserve Board, which raised interest rates six times. The Federal funds rate started the year at 3 percent and climbed to 5.5 percent by year-end. The change in interest rates unsettled the stock market and slowed the growth of the mutual fund industry. The Dow Jones Industrial Average increased 5.06 percent, the S&P 500 increased 1.36 percent, and the NASDAQ decreased 3.2 percent. The interest-rate changes also led to the worst bond market in more than 60 years.

Many fixed-income shareholders found, to their dismay, that after a decade of advancing bond prices, the market could also have a volatile downside. The situation was particularly alarming for former bank investors who were accustomed to holding certificates of deposit or, even worse, thought that the asset levels of their bond funds were guaranteed.

As AIM's director of investments, Gary Crum was responsible for recruiting and retaining quality portfolio managers during the 1990s bull market.

Although fund industry assets increased by $90 billion to $2.1 trillion during the year, it faced new challenges. When the news media reported that several fund managers apparently were trading for their own accounts using the influence of their position, the fund industry quickly responded.

Bob Graham was among the members of a blue-ribbon panel appointed by the Investment Company Institute to look into the individual trading practices of investment personnel. Strong recommendations were made, and the swift action was well-received by the SEC. Graham and other members of AIM's senior management team knew all too well that AIM had to remain at the forefront of such self-regulatory efforts by the fund industry in order to maintain AIM's unquestioned integrity.

While many other fund companies experienced an overall decline in sales in 1994, AIM's retail department reflected a modest increase. Much of the year was spent on diversifying a product line that added three new global funds – AIM Global Aggressive Growth Fund, AIM Global Growth Fund, and AIM Global Income Fund – and building corporate infrastructure. Demand for sales and marketing literature grew to such an extent that AIM's supply and distribution operation had to be relocated to a first-class, 30,000-square-foot distribution facility in the Garden Oaks area of Houston. When finished with his initial tour of the new distribution center, Ted Bauer proudly exclaimed, "Wow! There really is an AIM!" The facility had doubled in size as a result of the large volume of literature being distributed.

Continued growth also forced AIM to ponder other challenges, such as how the company would be able to react in the event of a devastating hurricane or other natural disaster along the Texas gulf coast. A 150-seat facility was developed in Denver that would enable AIM to continue its critical operations within 24 hours after a business recovery situation was declared. One year later, Austin was selected as the location of a second facility to service and process transfer agent activity. The close proximity to Houston was an important factor in selecting Austin because of business-recovery considerations and the importance of having transfer agent functions available to shareholders and dealers whenever the market is open.

"We also began to engage the company in an ongoing effort to achieve better name recognition, first through the consistent use of the AIM signature in our internal and external communications, and also through proactive

R. W. Baird exits fund business, sells to AIM

By TIME QUINSON
Bloomberg Business News

MILWAUKEE (NYT) — Robert W. Baird
& Co. is getting out of the business of managing
mutual funds about nine years after the ... of ...
brokerage firm's first f...

Baird is selling
mutual funds to H...
ment Group for a...
company said to...
expected to be comp...

"Compared wit...
firms, Baird doesn't...
network through whi...
funds and we don't ha...
our investment officer...
ary funds," said Ronal...
aging director at Baird.

Baird's 500 brokers
funds from other fund co...
ers, Kruszewski said. Ba...
to manage $1.5 billion fo...
vate investors. No staff re...
a result of the sale of the m...
he said.

Headlines from the
Orange (TX) *Leader* and
the *Houston Chronicle*.

AIM to buy three Baird funds

Growing company will gain nearly $137 million in assets

By CHARLES BOISSEAU
Houston Chronicle

AIM Advisors, the fast-growing
Houston mutual fund company,
announced Thursday it will buy
the assets of three funds from the
brokerage Robert W. Baird & Co.

AIM plans to rename two of the
Baird funds and add them to the
current lineup of 21 mutual funds,
said Ivy McLemore, spokesman
for AIM.

The other Baird fund being purchased, a bond fund, will be absorbed into a similar fund managed by AIM, he said.

The three funds AIM is buying
had assets of $137 million as of
Sept. 30. The sale is expected to be
completed in the spring after approval by Baird fund shareholders.

While the companies did not disclose financial terms, industry ex-

perts said the selling price of such
funds typically is about 2 percent
of assets, making this deal worth
about $2.7 million.

"It's a drop in the bucket for
AIM," said John Rekenthalen,
publisher of Morningstar Mutual
Funds, a fund research publica-
tion. Its database follows about
7,900 stock and bond funds nationwide.

Since it was founded in Houston
in 1976, AIM has grown to rank as
the nation's 16th-largest mutual
fund company with about $41 bil-
lion in assets under management
and 2 million shareholders.

The private firm has more than
tripled in size since 1992, when it
acquired a family of funds from
Cigna Corp. Its work force has
more than doubled to nearly 1,000
employees, all in Houston, in two
years, McLemore said.

For Milwaukee-based Baird, the
funds it is selling were a sideline

because the brokerage has a
small distribution network and its
brokers weren't required to sell
its funds, said Ronald Kruszewski,
managing director. The Baird
funds had about 5,000 shareholders, he said.

The funds likely will benefit
from the wider-reaching distribution network of AIM, which sells
its mutual funds through 100,000
brokers nationwide.

Specifically, the Baird Blue Chip
Fund, a growth and income fund,
will be renamed AIM Blue Chip
Fund—while the Baird Capital De-
velopment Fund, a small- and
mid-cap fund, will be renamed the
AIM Capital Development Fund.
The Baird Quality Bond Fund
will be absorbed by the existing
AIM Income Fund.

Rekenthaler said he was a bit
puzzled by the purchase of the
small funds, as none of them were
known as particularly outstanding
performers.

*AIM paid big dough for three Baird funds in 1996, then watched assets
rise from $137 million to more than $7 billion in less than four years.*

outreach to the financial press," Ted Bauer said. "While
the success of such efforts is always difficult to measure,
great strides have been made in recent years in increasing
public awareness of AIM as a mutual fund company,
thereby engendering brand loyalty."

A direct example of AIM's increasing name recognition was reflected in the decision to close AIM Aggressive
Growth Fund to new investors for the first time on May 2,
1994. Superior performance in the small-cap fund had
attracted the attention of financial advisors. The resulting
increase in net assets prompted AIM to close the fund to
preserve the best interests of fund shareholders in a
volatile small-cap market. Assets in the fund nevertheless
doubled to $312 million during the year as the fund
remained at or near the top of the list of top-performing
small-cap funds for the trailing five-year period.

Within a year, the overall environment for small-cap stocks had improved to the point that AIM believed it could reopen the fund to serve a dual purpose. First, it would enable the fund to take in new assets that would provide the fund's management team led by Bob Kippes to take advantage of new opportunities in small caps. Such opportunities had been limited because of a restricted cash flow in a fund that had been closed to new investors. Second, it would enable investors to buy shares of a small-cap fund with superior performance.

Original plans called for the fund to remain open for at least five business days with the goal of bringing in approximately $500 million in new assets. An announcement was mailed to financial advisors in June 1995 informing them of AIM's plans to reopen the fund for a limited period effective Monday, July 17, 1995. Midsummer traditionally is a slow time of the year for mutual fund sales, and AIM thought such a move might add a little spark in its marketing activity. No one could predict at the time that the fund's reopening would serve as a microcosm of the fund industry in the 1990s, jump-starting asset growth in what would prove to be a raging bull market of unprecedented proportion.

AIM was prepared for an increase in phone traffic the first day the fund was reopened to new investors, but the fund's overwhelming popularity was so great that it literally overloaded the company's phone capacity. So many brokers were placing incoming orders that phone lines were shut down for a brief time on a day when AIM still took 30,000 phone calls – more than 15 times the average phone traffic for a summer day at the time. Senior management quickly realized that the reopening had been such a blockbuster that its goal of raising $500 million in assets might be reached far sooner than planned.

"We didn't even know how much money we'd raised because we blew the computer at A.G. Edwards and couldn't get the numbers from everybody until late that night," Jim Salners recalled. "We didn't realize the magnitude of the situation until almost 10 the next morning when all the numbers were in and we learned we'd taken in more than $600 million the first day! That's when we went to everyone and said we'd have to shut it down at the end of the second day."

By the close of business on Tuesday, the reopening of AIM Aggressive Growth Fund had resulted in $1 billion in new assets, an industry record for a two-day period. "Our sales, on a weekly basis, had been averaging $150 million and there was no precursor to this," Salners said. "But it was a firestorm that really gave us a level of understanding as to how well-known we actually were. We took 110,000 orders and 52,000 phone calls in two days! Our sales averaged $250 million from that point forward for the rest of the year. We got $1 million worth of free press from the reopening alone. It's a lot easier to get more business out of somebody that's already selling your product than it is to go out and convince somebody new to sell it."

The reopening, in part, enabled AIM's growth to far exceed the industry average in 1995. AIM increased its net retail sales by 82 percent year-over-year, the highest such increase of any major fund company. "AIM was the leading market-share gainer for 1995 in our book," said Lou Harvey, president of DALBAR, a Boston-based independent mutual fund monitor. "They edged out American Funds, which had been the traditional leader in this (non-

AIM employees who participated in the reopening of AIM Aggressive Growth Fund in 1995 received a commemorative T-shirt. Left to right, marketing specialist managers Simon Hoyle (NYSE Division), Terri Ransdell (IIDD Division), and Scott Burman (FID Division).

proprietary) channel. It was quite a shock to see someone other than American Funds at the top of the heap."

T-shirts with the phrase *I Was There and I Survived* were given to all employees who participated in a landmark event that mirrored the success of financial markets in 1995. The NASDAQ increased 39.9 percent, the S&P 37.45 percent, and the Dow Jones Industrial Average 36.83 percent. AIM Aggressive Growth Fund was up 41.51 percent for the year, helping AIM finish third among 57 fund families ranked by *Mutual Funds Magazine* in terms of overall performance for the year.

With the industry in the midst of a growth phase, AIM continued to diversify its retail product line in 1996 with the acquisition of three funds from Robert W. Baird & Co. of Milwaukee. Northwestern Mutual Life Insurance

Company, Baird's parent company, owned 80 percent of the Baird funds. As a side benefit of the acquisition, AIM gained access to Northwestern's sales force of 3,500 financial advisors.

Two of the Baird funds AIM purchased were given the AIM name and renamed AIM Blue Chip Fund and AIM Capital Development Fund. The two funds had $76 million and $50 million in assets, respectively. A third fund with fixed-income assets of $8 million was merged into the existing AIM Income Fund. A technical difficulty prevented the assets of Baird Capital Development Fund from being transferred immediately into the new AIM Capital Development Fund. As a result, AIM seeded the fund and hired highly respected industry veteran Ed Larsen to serve as portfolio manager. AIM Capital Development Fund was launched on June 17, 1996, the same day Baird Blue Chip Fund changed its name to AIM Blue Chip Fund.

"With AIM Capital Development Fund, we're going to take those IPOs that look like they have a great long-term future and start buying them," Bauer said. "We do almost $100 million in commissions on an annual basis, which makes AIM one of the top generators of commissions on the Street. We're also one of the most well-respected firms. With AIM Blue Chip Fund, we're going to buy the leading companies in the world."

Bauer once again would be proven a visionary. He conceived the idea of the purchase of the Baird funds for a modest price tag of $3.6 million. In less than five years, the funds' combined assets would grow more than fifty-fold to about $7 billion. Jon Schoolar directed the management of AIM Blue Chip Fund for a short while before turning management of the fund over to a team led by Monika Degan. Larsen continued to manage AIM Capital

Development Fund until he was named chief equity officer in 1997 and turned day-to-day management of the
fund over to Paul Rasplicka.

"Ted Bauer did the Baird acquisition all on his own,"
recalled Roberto de Guardiola, who was instrumental in
AIM's purchase of the CIGNA funds in 1992. "He called
me up one day and said, 'I'm going to do this' and didn't
even ask me what I thought. I guess he wanted to prove
he could do a deal on his own."

By year's end, all three major market indexes – the
S&P 500, NASDAQ, and Dow – had achieved returns of
at least 20 percent for the second year in a row. Solid
fund performance and fine overall sales helped AIM
increase its assets under management by 50 percent to
more than $62 billion, helping the company climb from
17th to 12th among U.S.-based fund companies.

AIM made headlines as a result of the company's stellar
growth. During the year, AIM was rated No. 1 in terms of
equity performance by *Worth* magazine. In early 1997,
Barron's ranked AIM third among all fund families based
on 1996 performance in five diversified categories. AIM
also was profiled in such publications as *The Wall Street
Journal, American Banker, Forbes, Morningstar Investor,* and
Pensions & Investments.

Bauer also participated on a blue-ribbon panel of fund
industry executives at a Mutual Fund Forum symposium
in New York attended by more than 50 members of the
national media. Also during the year, Bauer wrote a guest
editorial that appeared in the *Houston Chronicle* and cau-
tioned shareholders against unrealistic expectations of
market performance. Bauer included a similar message in
the chairman's letter in AIM's fund shareholder reports.

Left to right, Monika Degan, Ed Larsen, and Craig Smith apply AIM's earnings discipline when selecting growth stocks for fund portfolios.

A raging bull market had helped put AIM in the right business at the right time, and people had taken notice. More than 26 million pieces of literature were printed and more than 860,000 phone calls were handled during the year. Nevertheless, senior management knew that great attention must be paid to continuing good investment performance and the ongoing expansion of corporate infrastructure if AIM was to sustain its growing momentum.

Chapter Sixteen

A MERGER
OF EQUALS

AIM's goals in the early 1990s had included the development of a broad and attractive product line, the acceptance of those products through diverse marketing outlets, and the establishment of a broad geographical base for product sales. To achieve the latter goal, AIM instituted an international effort in 1994 and selected chief legal counsel Bill Kleh to spearhead the project. Kleh was chosen, in part, because of the challenges AIM knew it would encounter with the diverse and, at times, arcane laws in the international arena.

Kleh was a vocal advocate of AIM's plans to expand overseas. He believed the direction of the fund industry was moving swiftly toward global money management and he wanted the company to be on the leading edge of that movement. AIM took its first step on a long, slow road to international acceptance by creating a dollar-denominated money market fund in Dublin, Ireland, to be run out of a newly established London office directed by Kleh. "If you had asked me in 1976 if I thought we would have global offices 20 years later," Bob Graham recalled, "I would have told you we'd have been lucky if we ever got outside the city of Houston."

AIM's initial plans called for Kleh to help bring to market liquidity funds as they were called in Western Europe and ultimately sell long-term investment products through its Irish facility. AIM's original dollar-denominated money market fund was called the Short Term Investments Company (Global Series) US $ Portfolio. The fund was domiciled in Ireland in November 1995 because of that country's favorable tax climate and the fact that Dublin banks had developed support capabilities for mutual funds both as custodians and as keepers of shareholder records. Assets of the fund increased dramatically in 1996 when Lloyd's of London was attracted as a principal customer. In 1997, AIM introduced a pound sterling money market fund in the United Kingdom.

In overseas meetings, Ted Bauer explained that AIM was trying to duplicate its domestic story in the international marketplace. "We started with money funds in the U.S.," he said. "We started with a very simple liquidity process that we understood and this market did not understand, and were going to grow from there."

From the outset, Kleh had more resources at his disposal in London than AIM had when it first opened its doors in Houston in 1976. "When we first started in London in 1994, we were in a managed office space of two offices in a West End suite between Berkeley and Grovesnor Square," Kleh recalled. "My office was right at the corner of a major intersection on the second floor, so it was noisy with buses turning all the time. My family had just joined me and it was very cold and rainy. We had this weekly conference call, where I would get on the phone with a bunch of people who were in a support role to international operations.

"On the first call, one of them asked, 'Well, Bill, how is it there in London?' I told them it was cold with a constant rain. I also told them we had high winds and bad pollution, trying to make it sound like I was at a real hardship post. Just then, the butler walked in and asked, 'Will you be having tea today?' All this time I'm trying to shoo him out of the room because it's a typical tradition to serve tea in London offices. Then the butler asks, 'And will you be having biscuits with your tea?'

"They were all laughing back in Houston. It sounded like I was having the life of a king when all they had when they started back in Houston was a card table and some folding chairs. But in reality, there were many days in London that I thought I was trying to move a wall of sand by leaning against it. Nobody in Europe had ever heard of AIM, so even if we had been trying to sell one of our wonderful equity funds like Weingarten or Constellation, it would have been an uphill struggle. Second, nobody had ever heard of money market funds."

AIM decided to add another dimension to its globe-trotting efforts in 1994 by forming an investment firm in Pakistan called ABAMCO Limited. "Karen Dunn Kelley's father had been a senior officer with Bear Stearns and had helped set up a joint venture for a broker/dealer in Pakistan to create a full-service investment firm there," Kleh said. "That joint venture was looking for a mutual fund manager to come in and assist them by creating a mutual fund group which would have been the first privately sponsored fund organization in that country.

Bill Kleh, AIM's chief legal counsel in the late '80s and early '90s.

The new operation was created in conjunction with an affiliate of World Bank called the International Finance Corporation, a Bear Stearns affiliate, the Moslem Commercial Bank, and AIM. Polly Ahrendts, a long-time member of AIM's fixed-income department and Leslie Schmidt, who had an operations and accounting background, were chosen to head AIM's new outpost in Karachi.

Kleh was to oversee the project from his London offices as president of AIM Global Holdings. "The thought of AIM going to Pakistan was like America going to the moon. It stirred people up," Kleh said. "Even people who aren't in that particular issue or in that process

Headlines from the *Financial Adviser*, the *Financial Times*, and *USA Today*.

The AIM-INVESCO merger created AMVESCAP PLC, one of the world's largest independent asset management companies.

become excited by being in a company that's doing that kind of stuff."

Then disaster struck. Political unrest once again began to bubble up in that corner of the world and hit uncomfortably close to home when two Americans were shot in Karachi on the day AIM was to close its joint venture. "When the Americans were shot, we decided not to put any of our people there at all because we did not want them at risk," Kleh said. As a result of the shootings, the original plans for Pakistan were scrapped and a Pakistani national was hired as a full-time employee to represent the company. One year later, the Pakistanis had their first open-end mutual fund.

Meanwhile, senior management also was looking to provide liquidity for common AIM stockholders, a search that could begin in earnest once Nationale-Nederlanden's clawback provision expired in June 1996. Under a clawback provision, firms must repay all or part of subsidies if they fail to deliver, under-perform or over-promise.

One option was for AIM to launch its own initial public offering (IPO), a notion that was quickly discarded. "We decided not to have an IPO because you have less flexibility than you have in a private company," Graham said. "We had been very fortunate that we hadn't had to worry about quarter-to-quarter earnings during AIM's first 20 years of operation. Once you're in a public environment, you have to become much more focused on managing your earnings."

In the quiet way that deals of such size are normally conducted, Roberto de Guardiola brought an interesting proposal to AIM's attention. He suggested AIM combine with London-based INVESCO PLC in a merger of two mutual fund companies that would create a platform for a global asset management juggernaut. INVESCO CEO Charlie Brady had never heard of AIM before de Guardiola mentioned the company as a possible merger candidate. "But it took me about 30 seconds to determine I wanted them," Brady said.

De Guardiola thought the cultures of both companies were similar. They had grown on different tracks, but each had been successful in its own right. "Our businesses complemented one other," Gary Crum said. "Obviously, we were interested in moving globally, and INVESCO had already established operations in Hong Kong, Tokyo, France and London, among other cities around the world. We had not. They also had a publicly traded stock, which was listed on the London Stock Exchange. We were in a position where we had taken a small amount of money out of our company over a period of years. Now it would be timely, we thought, to have this currency, a publicly held stock.

"We got together and talked to their people about our investment and management philosophies. What was truly unusual was that there was no overlap of personnel. This wasn't a situation where you had to come in with a set of 'rationalizations,' and lay off a bunch of people. We said at the time, no one would be laid off and, in fact, no one was. It seemed to be one of those ideal matches, where no one really gobbles up the other," Crum added. "You both stay intact, with one view and one personality. Our strengths were complementary, so that set a standard. INVESCO was larger in terms of assets under management, but we were actually the larger of the two companies in terms of earnings."

The complementary strengths of the two companies appeared to fit hand in glove. AIM had a strong retail presence in the broker/dealer community, a broad line of retail funds marketed through financial advisors, and a major institutional money market operation. INVESCO, meanwhile, had two primary businesses in the United States – a direct-marketed retail fund operation based in Denver and a separate, privately managed institutional account division in Atlanta. In addition, INVESCO had built a strong foundation for international operations and had strong 401(k) administrative facilities.

Of course, in any negotiation involving billions and crossing oceans requires a certain degree of secrecy and a higher level of diplomacy. "One of the things important to us was negotiating a deal where we received shares

Members of AIM's Legal and Compliance Department became specialists in M&A activity in the 1990s. Seated, Nancy Martin, Kathy Pflueger, Carol Relihan, and Sam Sirko. Standing, Tim Cox and Jeff Horne. Horne is now chief of staff for Bob Graham.

that would be exchanged at a fixed-dollar price," Crum said. "From our standpoint, the incentive was to keep it quiet because if the word got out, then their price would run up and we'd receive fewer shares. We had gone back and looked at the trading range on their stock from the previous 18 months. Their stock had been up slightly, but not by a great amount. And the market had been up by even more. It was our feeling that we were basically getting the shares at a price that was below the market."

Although the combination of the two companies made great conceptual sense, the technical implications of the proposed merger were enormous. Since INVESCO is a London-based company, representatives from AIM's legal, financial planning, and treasurer's departments faced unquestionably the most complicated transaction ever conducted in the mutual fund business. AIM's internal team

*Will Rheiner of the Philadelphia law firm of
Ballard Spahr Andrews & Ingersoll, LLP helped AIM forge
a final merger agreement with INVESCO.*

joined with outside legal firms, accounting firms, and
investment banking firms to negotiate terms with a like
INVESCO team. Essentially, they had to negotiate
through the maze of laws and regulations of two nations,
two regulatory bodies, two internal revenue services, and
two stock exchanges. In addition, financing had to be
arranged and issues of corporate governance resolved.

As is often the case with multibillion-dollar transactions, there were periods of tension and suspense. "There
were several times when we almost walked away from it,"
Crum said. "We were dealing from a position of strength
because we were making more money than they were.
We wanted it, and from several angles it made a lot of
sense, but if at some point things got irrational one way
or another, we would have just walked away."

The announcement of a merger transaction in which AIM and INVESCO would combine to form a powerful platform to face an increasingly competitive industry was made on November 4, 1996. The AIM Funds Boards of Directors/Trustees and fund shareholders had to approve the assignment of contracts to the new corporate structure. Will Rheiner, AIM's outside counsel and a true Philadelphia lawyer, tirelessly worked his way through a maze of legal challenges. He played an integral role in consummating the merger between the two companies on February 28, 1997, that created a holding company called AMVESCO. After a brief period, the name of the holding company was changed to AMVESCAP PLC for legal reasons.

"Technically, they acquired us," Bauer said. "But in real life we merged and created a new company. Since we were much bigger, they had to pay us cash before we swapped shares. We merged into them through one of the companies they have, and this allowed us to accomplish several things. We could have sold out to some European bank or even a domestic bank. Every underwriter wanted to take us public and that had a great appeal, to some degree. We wanted to be more liquid. We wanted to be global. We wanted our employees to have a way of obtaining stock. So the combination of these goals is what got us involved in this negotiation."

Original terms of the proposed merger called for AIM shareholders to be given $1.6 billion in a combination of stock and cash as total compensation for the company. The stock compensation was set at a peg price. By the time the deal was formally completed, INVESCO paid approximately $2.2 billion because INVESCO stock had appreciated from 37 to 50 in less than four months.

At the time of the merger, Brady became chairman and CEO of the new combined entity. The 15-member board was composed of seven INVESCO members and seven AIM members, with Brady having the 15th and potentially tiebreaking vote. However, a corporate governance was established under which Brady would be blocked from voting for anything that either the INVESCO or AIM directors unanimously opposed.

Bauer, Graham, Crum, and Mike Cemo joined the AMVESCAP board of directors. In addition, three non-management directors were selected by AIM – de Guardiola and former AIM board members Rod Canion and Steve West. Graham was named CEO of AMVESCAP's Managed Products Division, which is composed of AIM, INVESCO Funds Group in Denver, and AIM Funds Management in Canada. Graham, Crum, and Cemo also are members of AMVESCAP's Strategic Planning Committee.

AIM accomplished several goals with the merger, not the least of which was liquidity for company shareholders. It now had a global platform with which to offer a variety of investment products. It also could pride itself in being part of one of the world's largest independent investment asset managers at a time when the competitive challenges in the mutual fund industry continued to intensify.

Chapter Seventeen

IRRATIONAL
EXUBERANCE

Between the time the proposed AIM-INVESCO merger was announced and the time the merger was finalized, Federal Reserve Chairman Alan Greenspan delivered one of the more memorable speeches of the 1990s. Speaking before The American Enterprise Institute for Public Policy Research at a dinner in Washington, D.C., on December 5, 1996, Greenspan opened his remarks by referring to William Jennings Bryan's famed "Cross of Gold" speech delivered 100 years earlier at the 1896 Democratic National Convention. As he neared the end of his remarks, Greenspan said, "How do we know when irrational exuberance has unduly escalated asset values...and how do we factor that assessment into monetary policy?"

The phrase "irrational exuberance" would become a catchphrase for the remainder of the decade when describing the Fed's opinion of unparalleled gains in the

AIM's original home page at www.aimfunds.com was launched in 1996.

stock market. Before 1996, the U.S. stock market, as measured by the S&P 500, never had enjoyed an appreciation of more than 20 percent for more than two years in a row. That record ultimately was extended to five years in 1999 when the S&P 500 gained 21.04 percent.

But the yellow-brick road investors had come to enjoy in the late 1990s wasn't without potholes. The stock market responded turbulently to continuing turmoil in Asia when the Dow Jones Industrial Average dropped a record 554 points on October 8, 1997. Investors then rushed in and the Dow recovered to 7,908 by year-end. But the recovery was very uneven, and investors sought the comfort of stocks of large-cap stocks of major corporations. Small- and mid-cap stocks showed only modest recovery.

In the summer of 1998, the vast variance between large- and mid-cap stocks was compounded when Long-Term Capital Management, a global hedge fund, rocked the world's currency markets with arrogant and faulty

currency portfolio hedging with a fund presumably leveraged 25-to-1. That disaster, compounded by Russia's debt
default, roiled securities markets. A general flight to U.S.
Treasury bonds and highly liquid equity securities culmi-
nated on October 8, 1998, when the stock market
reached its low point for the year and the S&P was down
14.5 percent. Fortunately, the Federal Reserve's positive
action – lowering the Fed Funds rate three times – combined with positive action by U.S. Treasury loans to very
weak nations – helped equity markets rally strongly by
year-end.

While the overall market was showing remarkable
resiliency on a calendar-year basis in the late 1990s, AIM
continued to build its infrastructure in order to meet the
public's seemingly insatiable demand for investment
products. AIM maintained its rapid growth throughout
the decade while meeting the many challenges that come
with expansion and competitive pressures.

In 1996, AIM created a seven-person task force directed by Mark McMeans that led to the creation of the company's first Web site – www.aimfunds.com. One year
later, an Intranet was introduced for employees. During
its first three full years of existence, aimfunds.com would
receive numerous awards for excellence among Web sites
of mutual fund companies whose products are sold
through financial intermediaries. AIM's senior management believes the role of electronic commerce will
increase significantly in the early years of the new millennium as the Internet continues to transform many
aspects of business.

In addition to emphasizing the importance of the
electronic commerce, AIM escalated expenditures in

computer equipment and software in order to remain on the cutting-edge of the asset management industry. The Information Technology Department more than doubled in size from 1997-99 in a tight labor market for IT professionals. The growth of AIM's IT operations had become so intensive that network infrastructure had to be replaced under a program affectionately designated "Slash and Burn."

Among major initiatives, the Merrin trading system was developed for the Investment Department, the MARS system was developed for Retail Marketing, and AIMLink was developed for Institutional Marketing. Another major IT-related project involved the planning and execution of an off-site computer center for AIM's and AMVESCAP's future needs. Significant projects in 1998 included the launch of a Wholesaler Information Network, construction of a data center in downtown Houston, and a complete rebuild of AIM's computer network under the supervision of John Deane.

Enhanced technology was necessary in order for AIM to maintain a superior level of customer service greatly expanding its list of product offerings. As part of its ongoing international initiative, AIM began offering four equity funds and a strategic income fund to the non-resident alien market overseas under the AIM Capital brand. These five offshore funds, first offered in April 1997, were intended to help build AIM's international exposure. One year later, a pound-sterling money market fund was instituted by AIM Global and, by year-end, had more than $114 million in assets.

AIM also continued to launch new funds for U.S. investors in the late 1990s. "To further assure growth,

AIM must provide more products to meet the demands of the 401(k), 403(b), and 457 plan retirement markets as well as the wrap business," Ted Bauer said. "Some 40 percent of new mutual fund sales are aimed at those markets."

AIM European Development Fund and AIM Asian Growth Fund widened AIM's international scope. AIM High Income Municipal Fund broadened tax-free offerings. AIM High Yield Fund II increased the company's flexibility in managing high-yield assets. AIM Small Cap Opportunities Fund gave AIM its first true long/short product. AIM also launched such products as AIM Mid Cap Opportunities Fund and AIM Dent Demographic Trends Fund, sub-advised by best-selling author and market sage Harry S. Dent, Jr.

As an offshoot of the AIM-INVESCO merger, AIM also took over the marketing and distribution of seven INVESCO Advisor funds in August 1997. The seven funds had been sold by INVESCO through the use of Class C shares, and it was obvious to AIM and INVESCO that the funds could be more effectively marketed by AIM through its vast network of financial advisors. A small money market fund and a fixed-income fund were merged out of existence in early 1998, leaving five equity funds that helped broaden AIM's product line. Much of the integration was eased by the creation of a product management team in 1997 under the direction of senior vice president Marilyn Miller.

AIM was involved in a far more complex transaction in 1998 when AMVESCAP purchased the asset management division of the Liechtenstein Global Trust in June 1998. The transaction involved the acquisition of the 29

GT Global funds, all of which had been sold through third-party intermediaries. The GT Global funds had combined assets of approximately $8 billion and would almost double AIM's number of existing funds, but AIM was charged with the difficult task of trying to stem redemptions from the funds and properly integrate the former GT Global product line with The AIM Family of Funds®. Further, AIM personnel were asked to supervise the integration of the $2 billion Canadian operation into AMVESCAP's Managed Products Division.

For more than a year, the addition of the former GT Global funds adversely affected the perception of AIM's relative overall investment performance. When AIM's performance was measured by a simple arithmetic average of all funds, AIM dropped from its usual very high position to an unfavorable level. Nevertheless, on a dollar-weighted average, AIM's performance in 1998 placed it second only to Fidelity among the nation's 10-largest fund families in terms of assets under management as measured by the Boston-based firm Kanon Bloch Carre.

Within two years of its acquisition of the former GT Global funds, AIM had either merged or changed portfolio management on the vast majority of them. "Good investment performance is and must be a constant goal," Bauer said. "And expansion of corporate infrastructure is obligatory to meet the demands of both AIM corporate operations and our investment customers. The competitive challenges in the mutual fund industry continue to intensify and are imposing."

AIM continued to meet the challenges of the fund industry by adding Class B and Class C shares to virtually every fund in its retail product line. "There is an inces-

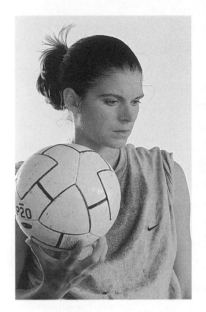

World-class amateur athletes Mia Hamm and Lance Armstrong
were featured in AIM's "Invest with DISCIPLINE®" ad campaign in 1999.

sant trend toward commissions in the industry away from the fund sponsor to the retail distributor," Bauer said. "The trend is in addition to the growing demand for financial sales support. For instance, in wrap accounts and retirement accounts, the fund is sold no-load and, in turn, the distributor receives compensation of commission or fees from the client.

Miller, AIM's director of marketing, was instrumental in AIM's product line expansion and accompanying increase in national exposure through an aggressive advertising campaign which used the tagline "Invest with DISCIPLINE®." AIM's branding program included a "Pop Quiz" campaign on cable television in 1998. One year later, AIM received accolades for its extensive television ad campaign that featured world-class amateur athletes Lance Armstrong and Mia Hamm and an avalanche of attention from its print ad campaign that trumpeted the fact that 29 AIM funds outperformed the S&P 500 in 1999.

Corporate branding also initiated a new corporate identity program launched under Mary Kay Coleman, AIM's director of marketing communications. Key features of the program included a change of the corporate color from burgundy to green to more closely reflect what the public sees in AIM's advertising and public event promotions. A little-known fact is that AIM consistently ranks second only behind the *Houston Chronicle*, the city's only major newspaper, in terms of print buying each year. In 1998, AIM's Marketing Communications Department produced 60 million units of 700 different literature pieces and was ranked No. 2 behind all fund companies in terms of effective sales literature.

AIM continued to receive top awards and recognition for fund performance from *Worth* magazine, *Smart Money*, and *Mutual Funds Magazine* in the late 1990s. In February 2000, *Barron's* rated AIM as the top-performing fund family over the trailing 10-year period, effectively crowning AIM as "The Fund Family of the 1990s." Media outlets picked up on AIM's superior performance, profiling such products as AIM Dent Demographic Trends Fund, AIM Value Fund, and AIM Aggressive Growth Fund in early 2000. "A sound media relations policy can achieve exposure that money cannot buy," Bauer says.

As part of its continued growth in the late 1990s, AIM took several steps to cope with the continuing tight labor market. In hiring, AIM's nepotism policy was relaxed for

AIM's equity trading area is the backbone of the company's Investment Department.

all but the families of very senior officers, and recruiting efforts were upgraded. To enhance employee retention, new benefits were implemented and old ones improved. Other initiatives included developing a new AFS incentive plan and improving performance-development processes for individual departments. "One of AIM's strengths over the years has been very low turnover of investment and key personnel," Bauer said. "As the industry grows, AIM must continue attending to staff continuity."

The first quarter of 2000 was one of the best three-month periods in AIM's history. AIM was among the top four mutual fund companies in terms of net flows into its retail funds, resulting in a flurry of activity.

McMeans, Kamala Sachidanandan, and Ann Srubar worked to help AIM enter the private asset business. Stephen Bitteker and John Cooper were hired by retail marketing to oversee AIM's offshore funds and retirement plans business, respectively. Bob Vansant and his staff continued to bolster AIM's presence in the variable annuity market. Ofelia Mayo and Michelle Grace of the legal staff kept busy stickering prospectuses as AIM added to its portfolio management teams. Brenda Thomas, Tom Severski, and Janet Henton of human resources worked diligently on recruitment and retention of employees in a period of low unemployment.

Rebecca Starling-Klatt and Beth Brown of AIM's Compliance Department made certain growing amounts of sales literature met NASD standards, while Dave O'Neil and his staff at AIM's distribution facility helped fulfill an average of almost 2,000 literature orders per day. Jay Wilson and his staff continued AIM's Business Recovery efforts in Austin to ensure uninterrupted service in the event of a hurricane or other calamity.

By June 2000, AIM had more than $176 billion in net assets under management, more than 7 million shareholders, and more than 2,500 employees. The little company that was launched under modest circumstances in 1976 had been bolstered by a rare combination of corporate vision and good fortune and an unparalleled period of exceptional exuberance by stock markets that helped push the total assets in the mutual fund industry to more than $7 trillion.

Chapter Eighteen

INVESTING IN PEOPLE

You hear a lot today about companies with heart. Some organizations use it as a way of luring employees in an increasingly complex society composed of Baby Boomers, members of Generation X and Generation Y, and people of varied backgrounds.

"I'm not sure we break with tradition," says Bob Graham, who succeeded Ted Bauer as CEO of AIM in February 1997. "I'm not sure we do anything other companies don't say they do, too. It's very popular these days to talk about how the employees are your most important asset. It's the standard thing to say. But we don't want work to be all-consuming to our employees. We don't want people working late out of fear that, 'Gosh, I've got to get this done or I'm going to get fired.' I don't know how you can have a successful career without having a successful personal life. You need that to support you in your career.

"Even back in our days at American General, Ted was the one who gave younger people like Gary Crum and myself a lot of opportunity – the kind of opportunity a lot of managers would not have offered inexperienced people like us. This may sound trite, but he's always cared for people. He wanted to be sure that they were treated with respect and took pride in their jobs and in their company."

Added Carl Frischling, AIM's outside legal counsel during the company's formative years, "Many, many years ago, Ted recognized the mutual fund business as a people business. Very few investment people understand that."

Bauer has a modest, uncomplicated view. "When I was CEO, I thought my biggest job was to create excitement. Everybody around me here is young. They're all ambitious. Most of them are highly educated. To build a company that is going to grow and be vital, you have to create excitement. I think that is one thing we did, all along."

If you ask how, Bauer leans back and laughs. "You start by having an atmosphere that's fun. I just remember that we had frequent parties to cultivate fellowship. The Christmas and other parties were often at my house. We had nametags, with the date each employee arrived and the size of AIM's assets at the time. My tag had a zero on it. So did Bob's and Gary's. It was fun just to show the progress of the company and it encouraged a family feeling."

The concept of hosting celebrations for AIM employees hasn't changed over the years. In 1996, the company held a 20th anniversary party for employees outside the company's headquarters at Greenway Plaza. Two years later, it held a celebration to commemorate the milestone achievement of having $100 billion in assets under management. In 1999, another celebration was held for all

Bob Graham, Ted Bauer, and Gary Crum discuss the recipe for AIM's success during the company's 20th anniversary employee luncheon.

employees in nearby Compaq Center in observance of AIM's $125 billion in assets under management.

Another popular gesture among employees is AIM's annual Holiday Gala, a festive tradition in Houston and Austin that has grown in size and stature. AIM traditionally serves more than 10,000 pieces of shrimp, 300 pounds of tenderloin, and 8,000 chocolate truffles to more than 2,000 employees and guests.

"If you're having a good time and you feel comfortable, everybody works like crazy," Bauer says. "Gary Crum came in one day in 1995 and said, 'If we get to $50 billion, we've got to get something for the employees at our next quarterly meeting.' So we ordered all these baseball caps with AIM on the front and a little emblem on the back. I said let's go ahead and give them out now because otherwise we'll be snakebitten and never get to $50 billion, so we gave them out when we hit $48 billion. Little things like that are fun."

In a 1997 interview with *Investor's Business Daily*, Bauer explained the attitude that helped transform an upstart company into one of the giants of the mutual fund industry.

"In the investment business, people are the product," he said. "Your inventory goes down the elevator every night, and comes back up in the morning. If you have people who are comfortable in their jobs and don't think they are being second-guessed at every moment, but are treated in a more mature fashion, they'll work harder and be more productive. If they're worried about their compensation, they don't work hard."

One of the ground rules AIM presented INVESCO when the two companies merged to form AMVESCAP PLC in 1997 was that no AIM employee would lose his or her job. "That was written in stone," Bauer said. Turnover at AIM's senior level has been almost nonexistent.

"In this business, two things are very important, Bauer says. "First, there's continuity of management. Investors want to see the same people year after year managing their money. Second, there's continuity of investment policy. People want to know precisely what you're doing."

Bauer's people-friendly mantra can be traced to his days in the military in World War II and his first few years in the business world. "I saw in my own history how long it took me to get anywhere," he says. "Therefore, I've always been particularly sensitive to the needs of others.

Although AIM long ago added its 2,000th employee to the company payroll, Bauer still finds time to greet newcomers at new employee orientation and cover what might be identified as the company's eternal truths.

*Bob Graham has continued AIM's reputation
as a people-friendly company.*

While some cynics may regard orientation as akin to jury
duty, Bauer gives it a high priority. It is a chance for new
hires to look him over; his to meet as many as he can.

"AIM's mission statement and principles of success are
pretty simple," he says. "When I meet with our new
employees at orientation, I talk about what business we're
in. Clearly, we're in the investment business. But I tell
them, 'You are now AIM. You are the voice on the telephone that people hear, so please conduct yourself
accordingly. Be nice to them. Sometimes you have to
accept some aggravation. You're on the firing line. You
can see things we never see."

Bauer also tells employees two things can get them in
trouble – breaking company rules or harassment. "We won't
stand for it. Male or female, makes no difference. People
who are comfortable in their jobs will work better than if
someone is trying to beat on them. If you ever have that

trouble, immediately go to your department head or to the head of human resources.

"The other thing I want them to know is that this business is the most supervised and regulated in the world with the possible exception of public utilities. If a utility wants to build a plant, it takes them 12 years to get regulatory approval. Here, it's every day. We have codes of ethics, and we want everybody to be his or her own compliance officer. If anyone thinks about cutting a corner, don't! We go through SEC rules. More than that, we want to have the world look at AIM as a highly ethical company.

"The history of the company takes half an hour. Most of them just sit back and don't ask questions. I say, 'Don't be bashful, just because I am. Ask questions.' On occasion, I get them going."

There are few companies more kid-friendly than AIM. "When I interviewed with Ted," says Judy Creel, "I remember saying, 'If this job requires a lot of overtime, I'm not prepared to do that right now. Our son is two years old.'

"Ted smiled and said, 'I understand. My son is four years old. If you need to work overtime, we will get you more help. Your family is important.' That's the kind of message we convey when we interview people. We want that good balance between work and family life."

There is no formula for hiring the ideal employee. AIM may put more emphasis than most on what does not appear in the job application: personality and fit. You can teach people the fundamentals of the industry – buy low, sell high – but it helps if they can think, react, and create. AIM looks for – and has done an admirable job of finding – an impressive array of self-starters.

"We used to say that we want to grow our talent from within," Creel says. "But as you expand, you have to go out and recruit some who have been successful elsewhere. You don't have time to cultivate them. We still prefer to promote from within, when we can. Even if we have headhunters out looking, or we've advertised in the trade journals, if we have openings we still post them in every department. We know that we have the talent to fill those jobs, if they want them."

AIM began quarterly employee meetings in 1988, when all employees could fit into one small auditorium. "I'm proud to work for a company that is willing to give incredible opportunities to capable employees who are looking for new challenges," Creel says. "Ted Bauer loves seeing employees who succeed in lofty goals, whether it's portfolio management or client service."

It has continued the tradition, even though the company's tremendous growth has prompted some employees to watch some of the presentation on closed-circuit television throughout the company. AIM prides itself on promoting a friendly, open environment. In addition, state-of-the-art technology is provided and ongoing career development training is made available to help employees reach their professional goals.

To recognize the entire workforce for its contributions in an important milestone, AIM observed its first business casual day in 1995 when the company reached $30 billion in net assets. A decision was made to observe a business casual day every time the company added another $1 billion in assets, a program that resulted in more than 100 casual days over the next five years. On

Mike Cemo and Abbott Sprague and their respective marketing divisions
serve thousands of clients between them on a daily basis.

January 1, 2000, AIM offered employees the option of wearing business casual attire five days a week.

"Having a casual day every time the company added another billion dollars in assets helped center the younger employees on how big the company was becoming," Bauer said. "And it created some excitement, because that's a CEO's job. You've got to create excitement if you're going to have young people, because if you don't, they'll go somewhere else. Young people want fun."

An example of how AIM employees enjoy a good corporate outing came in June 2000 during AIM Employee Appreciation Day at the inaugural season at Enron Field. More than 90 percent of AIM's workforce, including several busloads of employees from Austin, turned out for an Astros game against the Chicago White Sox.

Graham believes AIM offers a special type of spirit, one that was reflected in its first-ever recent employee survey in which 91 percent of the company's workforce said AIM was, indeed, a good place to work. "I think it has been beneficial for us to be in Houston as opposed to New York or Boston," he said. "I think you get a lot of wide-eyed kids here that think this is the greatest thing in the world and they have a job they enjoy.

"We believe that growth creates an exciting environment, a challenging environment for people and it's very important to have that type of situation in place. Once you've hired talented people with a lot of energy, you have to give them a chance to grow."

Chapter Nineteen

COMMERCE, COMMUNITY
AND CULTURE

At orientation meetings for new employees, Ted Bauer emphasizes the importance of taking pride in AIM and the community. "We want them to take interest in their church or synagogue, participate in the Boy Scouts, the Girl Scouts, or any good cause," Bauer says. "They will enrich their lives and secondarily make AIM proud because our company gets better known."

As AIM grew in corporate stature in Houston in the 1990s, so did its visibility in the community. AIM joined forces with the Galleria Chamber of Commerce in 1996 to launch the inaugural AIM Business Expo, which has since grown into the Greater Houston area's leading business-to-business showcase with hundreds of exhibitors and thousands of attendees each year.

The AIM Business Expo offers hundreds of local businesses the opportunity to meet potential clients and hear

*Ted Bauer receives a proclamation from Houston mayor
Lee Brown at the AIM Business Expo.*

successful business tips from prominent speakers. It also
features the latest advances in technology and services
that can assist the business community with potential
solutions to improve performance and production, stream-
line operations, and provide service needs inherent to
profitable day-to-day activities.

One of the important byproducts of the AIM Business
Expo has been the creation of The Houston Metropolitan
Study, an idea originally conceived by AIM in May 1996.
In the first major collaborative effort between Rice
University and the University of Houston, The Houston
Metropolitan Study is an ongoing, independent project
designed to identify and address the issues that will
define success for the City of Houston and surrounding
region in the 21st century.

Although the energy sector and space exploration
have brought Houston worldwide notoriety, specific

challenges must be met for Houston to be truly identified as a world-class city. AIM was well aware that Houston, with its unique entrepreneurial personality and continually changing character, has the ability to become one of the world's leading metropolitan centers. The Houston Metropolitan Study represented the rare opportunity to foster broad and genuine grassroots ownership of the project.

With AIM's assistance, and under the stewardship of the Galleria Chamber of Commerce, The Houston Metropolitan Study was organized around what Rice University and the University of Houston determined to be the five most important areas of focus for local decision-makers and the general public in the coming years:

- Social Integration and Diversity
- Human Capital and Workforce Preparation
- Infrastructure
- Urban Amenities
- Governance and Regional Decision-Making.

The Houston Metropolitan Study also outlined three factors essential in order for Houston to continue its growth into a great global metropolis:

- Houstonians need a good understanding of the new model of urban growth that has emerged in the late 20th century and what it portends for the future if metropolitan regions are to preserve and enhance their viability.
- Houstonians also need an understanding of the specific strengths the Houston region brings into a fast-changing world and how they can be cultivated more effectively.

*Patricia Lewis, left, has helped The AIM Foundation
receive high marks for its work with Wharton Elementary.*

- Houstonians must make an equally honest inventory of their deficiencies in this new world marketplace and develop policies that address them as efficiently as possible.

Among the ongoing study's major findings has been the realization that special emphasis must be given to Houston's recent immigrant populations and their children, who could become a new urban underclass unless their levels of educational attainment and job skills are improved. As an example of the importance of this process, AIM has adopted an elementary school in the Houston Independent School District with a strong track record and a clear commitment to serving students.

For the last decade or so, the community surrounding Wharton Elementary in the Montrose area about one mile west of downtown Houston has been predominantly low-income. Many of the children come from homes where Spanish is the primary language, and about a quarter of them come to Wharton without knowing English at all.

Wharton has met its challenges better than most Houston schools – its students are some of HISD's best performers academically. High expectations, a caring staff, and a supportive community are a few of the reasons. Wharton has done a lot to help its kids succeed, but as a small school with shrinking enrollments, it hasn't been able to provide an arts program for many years. AIM already had strong relationships with local arts organizations, and the company brought these groups to Wharton to help build the school's arts program.

"Many Wharton families can't afford art materials, musical instruments and museum admissions," said school principal Monica Sandoval. "Their lives are so enriched by what AIM has brought."

Some of the groups AIM has introduced at Wharton include:

- The Museum of Fine Arts. The MFA has provided curriculum kits and art resources for teachers, and the fifth-graders took three days of art classes at the museum.
- The Children's Museum. AIM worked with the museum to put on a Family Fair at Wharton, where parents learned inexpensive, creative, and educational activities they could share with their kids at home. Kindergarten students later guided their parents through the museum.
- The Houston Ballet. Fourth-graders attended two ballets during the first year of AIM's affiliation with Wharton – "The Nutcracker" and "Sleeping Beauty." Houston Ballet Academy students visited the students before each performance.

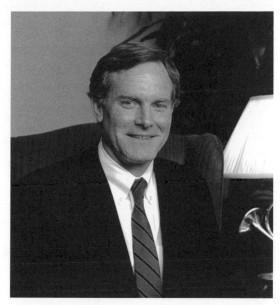

AIM annually plays host to the Carl Stevens Memorial Golf Tournament in Connecticut. The charitable event, which benefits ALS research, includes 180 investment professionals representing many of the nation's leading fund companies and financial institutions. Stevens, a wholesaler for AIM's Retail Marketing Department, died in 2000.

Chapter Twenty

THE END OF
THE BEGINNING

While the words "explosive growth" describe AIM's development in the 1990s, one word sums up how the company has survived and thrived during its first quarter century.

Change.

From the very beginning, AIM's founders were able to see changes in financial markets and capitalize on them by modifying the company's product line to meet the times. When they realized that managing private accounts was no longer lucrative, they created a money market fund to sell to institutions. When interest rates started to fall, they realized that fixed-income funds wouldn't be enough to sustain long-term corporate growth and they added equity funds to their fund family.

To provide a simple investment vehicle for those in the armed forces, the founders added contractual plans.

When they had no sales, marketing, or operations staffs, they created them. When investors wanted tax-deferred investment products, they bought the CIGNA funds and also added a line of variable annuity products and more equity and fixed-income funds.

As the world turned more toward international investing, AIM set its sights on opening offices in Pakistan and London and added international and global funds to its product line. When the company needed money, it took on financial partners, assumed debt, and reorganized. And, most importantly, when AIM made mistakes, the company lived through them and moved forward.

"The toughest thing about this business is catching the turn," Ted Bauer says. "That's why I don't dwell in the past. I always look toward the future. I'm excited to come to work in the morning.

"I'll tell you one thing about the investment business: If you're not learning every day, you're in trouble. It's a new business every day. Things that happen in South Africa will affect securities or what happened in New Hampshire yesterday will affect securities. What a vital business! What's a more exciting place than Wall Street?"

What does the future hold for the year 2000 and beyond? "The biggest danger in this industry is the performance we've had since 1990," Bauer says. "People have made fortunes. History shows that investors have benefited from growth of about 8 to 10 percent a year, but people have become accustomed to returns of 20 and 30 percent. That becomes exponential and you just can't have it. We try to dissuade fund shareholders from this pie-in-the-sky thinking through our annual and semiannual fund reports and other communications.

"Are there changes coming that will have a huge or important impact on this business in the years to come, in the banking and securities laws? The question is a rhetorical one. First of all, I'm no expert. I just have vague feelings. I think that banks are now mutual funders. They have to do it through a holding company, not the bank, but some of them are going to be very successful. First Union, Bank America, probably Chase, maybe Citicorp. They already have the power. So that will happen.

"Then, outfits like First Union are buying up companies. They have the financial clout to do it. As a result, one way or another, there are going to be fewer mutual fund companies, and fewer major players, because of the amount of money it takes to develop the infrastructure you must have to run a company.

"Some think of AIM as an in-house investment company, with a few outside investments. That's not it. We have more than 2,500 employees and maybe 10 percent of them are in the investment business. We have more than 700 people in shareholder services. The customer, the broker, has to be able to call up and get problems solved right away. The broker has one thing to sell: time. And in that time, he wants to create more commissions.

"As a result, we developed a Web site on the Internet – www.aimfunds.com – so every customer can call in to get his or her share holding and a complete list of transactions for the last two years on a day-to-day basis. The pricing comes up daily, morning, noon or night. Of course, that costs money.

"You have to have people sitting on the telephone all day long to answer the brokers' questions and those of the individual shareholders. You have to develop systems.

Bob Graham will succeed Ted Bauer as chairman of AIM
at the end of 2000.

Ours wasn't very good. In fact, at one point it was terrible. In 1999, we were recognized as one of the top nine out of 80 firms providing customer service. You spend a lot of money doing that.

"We have a system that allows your equity managers to call up anything in order to get breakdowns of the shares, the what-ifs, all that sort of thing. They must have this tool so they can be really effective. They need it to compete. In the money market area, we developed our systems to help our traders buy commercial paper. They can call up, say, General Motors Acceptance Corporation on their screens and they can find out which of our many funds own GMAC. The programs won't accept an order if they own too much GMAC, or too much of the industry, or if there is no money in the account.

"As soon as the deal is done, it prints out a ticket – who was the dealer, who was the trader, the immediate discounts and accruals of the interest. Then we fax that transaction to State Street Bank or the Bank of New York, depending on the custodian. Only then do we get a payment. We do billions and billions of dollars a day in money markets. You have to have systems.

"You also must have different systems for different parts of your businesses. You need them for private accounts, all the rest of it, as well as the securities firms. Then you need to have human-resource systems. We have well over 2,000 people in our Houston offices. We must constantly ask ourselves a variety of questions. How competitive are we? Are we losing people? How are we going to meet the demands for more information? You have to have systems!

"We are not just an investment company. You have to have fund accountants. They have to determine every night the pricing of the fund, which shows up in the newspaper. There is no room for error. There is an accrual of that day's income or that day's expenses. They have to turn it in by 4 o'clock in the East, and the markets may have closed at 3:30. For the banks, you have to be open later because they want to move monies later. And you have to be equipped to handle that flow of cash into the late markets. The world is also moving toward after-hours trading of equities. Life just becomes more and more complicated and the flow of information more accelerated.

"We have a large legal and compliance staff. We check every trade every day to be sure it is in compliance. If I want to make a personal transaction, I don't just do it. I go to the compliance department and ask, "May I buy this?' They will check the funds. Is anybody else buying it? Is there a conflict? If I do buy, and a fund manager buys

Ted Bauer: "People are the product."

within seven days – even if they were thinking about it for a longer period – I have to disgorge any profit I have in that because we must have integrity above reproach. We are dealing with other people's money. If you are not highly ethical, it will get around the Street. You can count on it. So when all of these things come together, what you have is the most complicated business the mind can conceive.

"Someday, we are going to have a tremendous correction in the markets. It's long overdue. But there is a reason why this market has gone on and on. There used to be something called inventory cycles. Today, you don't have that much inventory. Everybody has computer programs that track inventories, and the buyer constantly forces back inventory on the supplier. So everybody is running skinny because they figure, 'Well, I can get this stuff in a hurry because it's all in the computer.'

"Efficient portfolio managers were once a bunch of professors. They would talk about portfolio insurance. In the 1987 crash, their theories were absolutely blown away. Why? Because professors don't understand markets. Technically, on an even playing field, in a just world, they are right. But in a bad market, with over-the-counter securities, the market makers 'wind up in the men's room.' There is no market. Who are you going to sell it to, *The Wall Street Journal?*

"You can't rely on theory. I've warned our managers that they can't think there is going to be a market out there forever. I don't necessarily believe it. We discuss cash positions and portfolios for that reason. Faith and patience. Look at what is happening inside the company and don't get panicky because the market is going up or down. Are we providing a good service? That's when you have to hang in there.

"Our customer is the broker, the banker, the planner. He thinks he's buying a strategy. If we keep doing the same thing, year after year, ad nauseum, he never has uncertainty, he never has surprises. The market is down, he knows it's down, but if we follow the same strategies, he's comfortable. That's why we emphasize that it's important for us, and for others, to invest with discipline."

It's only fitting that we leave the final words of AIM's 20th century existence to co-founder Ted Bauer, who not long ago delivered the commencement address at Boston's Roxbury Latin School, his high school alma mater. And this is part of what he told them:

The Roxbury Latin School salutes Ted Bauer and his philosophy of 'carpe diem.'

"There is no true happiness without health, and no success without ethics. My favorite phrase is, 'For every forward-looking man, there are a thousand self-appointed defenders of the past.'

"If you are bold and eschew the mundane, you can become leaders. So far as I know, we only come this way one time. Give yourself a chance. Meet the challenges. Enjoy the excitement that comes with accomplishment. Pay the price. Allow yourself to dream. Give your dreams a chance to come true.

"And when you are firm in your convictions, don't let others tell you it can't be done."

Epilogue

OTHER VOICES,
OTHER ROOMS

T*he following is a collection of random thoughts and reminiscences from various AIM employees...*

BOB ALLEY
CHIEF FIXED-INCOME OFFICER

I was fortunate to join AIM in 1992 and watch the growth of a fine small company into a significant player in the global financial services business. I was impressed by the character and vision of the senior management team of Ted Bauer, Bob Graham, Gary Crum, and Mike Cemo. The culture of AIM always has been optimistic and opportunistic. Choosing talented employees and supporting people has nurtured an atmosphere of loyalty and excitement about the future. Mr. Bauer has framed this issue by saying, "People are the product."

Chief equity officer Ed Larsen, left, and chief fixed-income officer Bob Alley personify AIM Funds' tagline "Invest with DISCIPLINE®."

Vision, integrity, entrepreneurial spirit and perseverance have been personality traits that allowed the company to grow and to be successful. Good investment principles valuing discipline, diversification, risk control and continuity provided the foundation for our growth. The commitment to being a "first-class" provider of financial service products that satisfy our client's objectives is our focus and our future.

The merger with INVESCO in 1997 provided for a broadening of our product offerings, expanding our global business, and supporting the needs of the merged companies by enhancing our technology infrastructure that facilitates the investment process and our client service activities. Our desire to remain an independent company requires us to be responsive to opportunities to profitably grow our money management business across the globe.

*Bob Kippes, Ryan Crane, and Paul Rasplicka of
AIM's small-cap portfolio management team.*

I believe the soul and compass of AIM remains based on the wisdom and vision of Ted Bauer. A very valuable talent of an exceptional leader is the ability to develop the decision-making skills of the people who will take the company forward in the years ahead. In this regard, the future of our company appears bright.

Eva Bencze
Corporate Secretary –
Legal and Compliance

Picture this — The subsidiaries of a local investment company have 72 employees working on one-half of a floor in a high rise building that includes a "dungeon," which was really a hallway that housed most of the company files at the time. Assets under management are just over $7 billion. Industry assets are $716 billion, and there are less than 1,000 funds available nationwide. Three funds – Weingarten, Constellation, and Charter – have recently been acquired.

Imagine doing your work on word processors and typewriters, with no voice mail, e-mail or Internet. In

addition to normal workloads, you might be called upon
to help other departments during peak demand periods –
such as the crash of October 1987 – or calling shareholders when the return of proxy materials was lagging.
Needless to say, department staffs were rather small by
today's standards. For example, there were three employees
in Shareholder Services, two attorneys, six secretaries,
and a few accountants.

You always knew immediately when assets had increased by a billion dollars – the investment department
cheered and the red strobe light went on. Abbott Sprague
sported a variety of hats to let us know what was happening at the moment. When the company's anniversary
rolled around, we shared cake and champagne and the
photographs of AIM's beginnings were brought out –
including the one with the folding card table, with one
phone and the co-founders.

Like so many of my new co-workers, I had been
through the boom and bust of the oil industry and we
were ready for new excitement. It was, and remains, an
exciting industry full of opportunities...and AIM remains
a place to call home.

MARY BENSON
ASSISTANT FUND CONTROLLER

I joined AIM in 1985 almost straight out of Texas
A&M by responding to a newspaper ad. I remember one
year when the Christmas party was held after work in the
Investment Department of the 19th floor. At the time, the
entire company took up only one-half of the 19th floor.
To look at how huge the party is now, it's hard to imagine.

AIM had 60 employees when I was hired. In our department, I think we had four fund accountants and one supervisor and shareholder services consisted of four people. In fund accounting, we did money market funds and domestic common stock funds – international investments were not even a thought at that point.

When I look at the type and complexity of the investments now and the challenges that we and the company face everyday, I have great respect for all those involved, both in building the foundation of this company and maintaining the quality.

When I started with the company, most people did not know what a mutual fund company was. When I said I worked for AIM, they would say "Oh! You work for the toothpaste company!" I would patiently try to explain what a mutual fund was and what AIM was, but with some people – even my mother for a period of time – it was easier to say, "Yeah, the toothpaste business is doing great!"

Dick Berry
Senior Portfolio Manager – Tax-Free Bonds

I worked the first five years with AIM out of the Dallas office with Julian Lerner managing tax-free funds, a few private accounts, and the intermediate fund, which was small. In 1992, when AIM bought the CIGNA funds, Ted Bauer asked me to move to Houston.

When I first joined AIM, all of the furniture was used furniture that was bought at auctions as the small firms went out of business. As we took over office space, we moved things around without moving walls. A relaxed attitude and a good flow of information have helped AIM

Joel Dobberpuhl, Evan Harrel, and Rob Shelton of AIM's large-cap blend team, which manages the $30 billion AIM Value Fund.

grow. It encourages creativity. AIM is the only place I've worked where I really haven't had someone looking over my shoulder and second-guessing investment decisions.

Ted, for example, never spends all day in his office. He's constantly walking around the building, talking to people, finding out what's going on. As a result, a rapport develops that a lot of companies don't have. And if people enjoy what they're doing and feel like they're accomplishing something, that's got to carry over to their personal lives and make them happier people.

We're probably more rigid on regulatory compliance than anyone around. Certainly more than any firm I've worked for. That's a major benefit to shareholders, because it's a business of trust. As money managers, we have to keep reminding ourselves that it's not our money. It's someone else's.

The thing that has impressed me the most about AIM is the loyalty of the people at the top. Stick by them and they stick by the employees. That's probably the reason we've hardly had any turnover in the investment area. I think there were some 70-odd employees when I came in and now we have 2,500 or so.

*Claude Cody, Craig Smith, and Meggan Walsh comprise
the equity management team on AIM Balanced Fund.*

In the fall of '87, our equity funds got hit pretty hard, with a combination of the market decline and redemptions. We were able to withstand it and the performance came back fairly strong. The nice thing about being in this company, it was the first place I've worked as a fund manager where no one looked over my shoulder, which is great. Any fund manager is going to have a rocky year or two. Hopefully, not too many, but you're going to have periods where you stumble, and no one ever said a negative word to me.

Another advantage is that there is very little bureaucracy here. We have some now because we're a lot bigger, but it is nothing compared to when I used to work at the bank. At banks, your relative importance means how many meetings you can call and then actually avoid them. Here, I have one meeting a week with my department for thirty minutes every Monday, for communications mainly, so everyone will know what they are doing. We are blessed with a lot of self-starters. They don't need much supervision. They know what they can do.

I think the fact that we have so many young people, who are bright and aggressive and without fear, is one of the reasons we've done so well. You can argue it either way, but in this business, boldness usually wins out over caution.

JUDY BROWN
MANAGER OF PAYROLL AND BENEFITS

When I started at AIM, in 1990, there were just under 100 employees. I was the office administrator, i.e., a jack-of-all trades. I was responsible for payroll, the 401(k) paperwork and, believe it or not, facilities.

In the middle of preparing payroll or performing profit-sharing calculations, we might have a real emergency – a delivery of toner, or better yet, a plumbing problem. I worked for Judy Creel, who had hired every employee at that time. Judy personally delivered all the payroll checks. As part of my training to take over this task, I followed her to our new space on the 18th floor with a pad of paper and a pen to sketch the layout of cubicles. This chart had each person's name on it, in the proper cubicle order, so that I could assign a "payroll sequence number" for each paycheck. This would make it easier to pass out the checks since I did not know everyone by sight, as Judy did.

Julie Bell was my first hire and worked as our Payroll/Benefits assistant. Our payroll system at that time was a stand-alone personal computer with a modem to transmit the payroll to the service bureau. Julie had to pick up the modem and hold it at just the right angle in order to transmit the payroll information. Every night, I backed up the Human Resources system on tape and locked it in a fireproof file cabinet.

Charles Scavone, Ken Zschappel, Chris Perras, Rob Leslie,
Brant DeMuth, and Stephen Brase are portfolio managers
on AIM's opportunities series of funds.

BOB CHERICHELLA
REGIONAL SALES MANAGER/EAST, NYSE DIVISION

In the spring of 1990, I was job hunting and looking to align myself with a mutual fund company rather than the partnership business that I had been in for the past eight years. A very good broker friend of mine, Bert Herzog of Brighton, Michigan, told me that he was going to contact AIM mutual funds to try to arrange an interview for me through his wholesaler, Doug O'Dell.

I mentioned to Bert that I had never heard of AIM and he countered naming Weingarten and the Charter Fund. I told him that I thought that they were no-loads. He said to me "Bob, they are broker-sold and they are going to be The American Funds of the '90s." I owe a lot to Bert Herzog and Doug O'Dell.

After being hired as a banking wholesaler and being with the company just a few weeks, I attended my first sales meeting in Houston. There were 12 wholesalers in the company. Our sales meeting was held around a conference table – kind of different than our meetings today! Just as important back then were the sales ideas that we all shared during the course of the meeting.

At my first meeting, Gordon Sprague got up to share an idea with us that was working real well in rootin'-tootin' Texas. He started his presentation by firing a starter's pistol into the air. Now I have to admit that a pistol going off in a small conference room is startling.

Unfortunately, Bill Watlington was sitting next to Gordon when he fired the pistol. For those people who didn't know, or never met Bill, he had been an officer in the Marine Corps and took none too kindly to a civilian discharging a weapon in close proximity to his head. As I listened to some of the suggestions Bill was making to Gordon, I began to question the sane world of mutual funds as opposed to those crazy partnerships.

The early days of being a banking wholesaler were a challenge. With starting up a division at the same time Iraq invaded Kuwait, interest in selling equities was virtually nil in bank brokerages across the country. Weekly sales were measured in thousands, not tens of thousands.

The brokerage division had just started a focus with Weingarten in Merrill Lynch and Jim Salners had requested through John Frame, my boss, that I cover some Merrill offices for Doug O'Dell who had been called up to active duty in the Marine Corps. I guess that I enjoyed enough success that Jim asked John if he could talk to me about carving out a territory in the broker division. At the time, my territory accounted for a substantial part of banking's overall sales. John's reply to Jim was "That move would be good for Bobby, good for the company, and bad for me. Two out of three isn't bad." I owe a lot to John Frame.

Calling on wirehouses with mutual funds that were performing the way that ours were in 1991 was an entirely new experience for me. Having spent eight years selling partnerships, I was delighted to have products where brokers actually sought you out to hear about them.

I was in a Prudential office in Lansing, Michigan, my first month representing the NYSE division. As I was walking through the office, a broker that I knew from my old partnership days, came out of his office with his earpiece still attached and wanted to know if I was now "the Weingarten guy." He told me that he didn't have time to see me now, but wanted to know if he could buy me a beer at the close of the market! What a novel concept! I owe a lot to Jim Salners.

Every sales call that you made the first six months of 1995, no broker wanted to talk about how well the Value Fund was doing or that International Equity had rebounded nicely or that Constellation was doing so very well. All that they wanted to know was whether or when we were going to reopen Aggressive Growth. When word was leaked that the fund was going to reopen in July of that year, it was very apparent to me that interest in the reopening was going to be far greater than management could anticipate.

I have never been shy with expressing my opinion of what was happening in the field, and shared my thoughts

Ed Larsen, Lanny Sachnowitz, and Harry S. Dent, Jr., are the braintrust behind AIM Dent Demographic Trends Fund. Sachnowitz serves as lead manager and Dent as sub-advisor to the fund, which grew to $1.5 billion in assets one year after its 1999 launch.

on more than one occasion with Mike Cemo. In our early conversations, Mike felt that my estimates of sales in Aggressive Growth were "ridiculously optimistic." Within a couple of days, Mike realized that maybe the guys in the field had a pretty good handle on what was about to happen to the fund.

I kid Mike to this day about a voice mail that we got telling us to de-sell the reopening of Aggressive Growth. I've always scratched my head about that one. Mike was man enough to admit that he "kind of underestimated" the interest in the reopening, but managed to keep it open long enough that we did not burn any bridges in the brokerage community. I owe a lot to Mike Cemo.

STUART COCO
CHIEF FIXED-INCOME RESEARCH OFFICER

In 1988, AIM had about 100 employees. I was looking around because First City had changed senior vice presidents five times. So I didn't see that they were long for this world. Sure enough, about two years later they closed their doors.

Monika Degan, Rob Shoss, and Geoff Keeling of
AIM's large-cap growth management team.

I saw a lot of opportunity at AIM. What attracted me
was being able to come in as an analyst and portfolio
manager. I was the second one hired and then there was
a whole money market analytical staff because that was
the primary business then. I didn't have anything to do
with that, but I could see these guys were having a lot of
fun. I interviewed with Gary and Ted and with what seemed
like a dozen people. I just remember that we were laughing and having a good time. And I really felt like I had
connected with them.

Gary told me from the first day, "Stuart, I really can't
tell you what you will be doing next year, but I can assure
you there will be plenty of it to do." You just find out
what turns you on and that, more than anything else,
always has been the attitude here. That is what I've done.
The best part of it is, the three people who founded this
company have never changed. They are still having fun.
And they want you to pick up on it. That's cool. This is
like heaven that way.

It's such a simple formula. Hire good people and get
out of their way; let them do what they are good at doing.
It has paid off in a big way. Ted, Bob and Gary have kept
their word and, in this business, I can tell you that is more
valuable than bonds.

MARY KAY COLEMAN
FIRST VICE PRESIDENT/MARKETING COMMUNICATIONS

I joined AIM in March 1995 from Transamerica Funds. AIM was taking off just as two other local fund companies were closing shop after being acquired by John Hancock and Van Kampen, respectively. It was mutually advantageous to all parties. AIM needed experienced mutual fund people to meet the growing demands for expertise in virtually every area of the company.

What I suspect amounted to more than 100 displaced persons needed jobs. What a joy it was for us to come to a company that was succeeding! I was excited when Gary Littlepage called to ask me to interview for my position. I believe I was employee seven hundred and something and we had assets under management of $47 billion.

My most memorable moments have been working on the communication plan for the INVESCO merger, helping expand the quarterly employee meeting format, the 20th anniversary party and $100 billion party, and the first reopening of AIM Aggressive Growth Fund.

The growth of the company has so far exceeded my expectations, that I cannot imagine where it will stop. It definitely has come as a result of great leadership from the top, plus such catalysts as Mike Cemo, portfolio managers, and competent department heads across the board.

The mutual fund industry is one of the key industries to be in and AIM is the place to be in this industry. Young employees should learn everything they can and build a career based on that knowledge.

JUDY CREEL
DIRECTOR OF CORPORATE RESOURCES

In 1971, I left Pennzoil for a better job, with Funds, Inc., which later became Criterion and then John Hancock. That's how I got in the mutual fund business, and I stayed there for eight years. I knew there was another fund group downtown and that sort of piqued my interest because they were a young, start-up group. The company was AIM.

I was hired in 1979 as AIM's 16th employee. At Funds, Inc., I started off as a secretary to the vice president of finance, and worked my way up to corporate secretary. I had done legal liaison work, and handled all the printing for annual reports and the like. I came in for my first interview at AIM when Ted Bauer was out of town, and met with Bob Graham and another officer.

I think we sort of agreed that they couldn't afford me right then because they only had about 14 people. But they called back a couple of months later and said Ted was in town, and asked if I could come down and interview. We had a great rapport. Ted knew my boss and he said, "Why don't I call Tom and tell him you're coming to work for us?"

Until that point, a part-time student had been doing the state registrations, known as blue sky work, the filings to sell the company's offerings. I had supervised that as part of my duties at Funds, Inc., and that was to be my job at AIM. The scope was much less than what I was leaving, but I just had a great belief that this group would be going places. You felt a tremendous integrity.

When I came to work we had $125 million under management and there were only three mutual funds at the time. About that time, we brought out a short-term

Dave Barnard, Abel Garcia, and Bret Stanley. Barnard and Garcia are specialists in domestic technology and telecommunications stocks. Stanley is portfolio manager of AIM Basic Value Fund.

investments fund, and we sort of began to see that we had somewhat of a niche. I worked on that product and it confirmed what was so good about this place. The more willing you were to raise your hand and take on responsibility, the more they were willing to say, "Please do it." Some days your plate was way too full, but it got done.

I started handling the printing, doing the liaison work with Bob Graham, with the lawyers in New York. I arranged the meetings for the Board of Directors. I mean, whatever needed to be done, I wanted to do it.

About 1984, we began to pick up the pace a little in our hiring and that is when I became more involved. I also did some office management, working with the facilities. Then in 1986, we found a name for what I was doing, director of Human Resources.

So as the corporation grew, I was allowed to grow with it, which makes a job pretty wonderful. I have feeling for this company that is close to love. I have a lot of pride in the story, and I love telling the story. You do that anytime you hire someone. We have never been the sort of company that just hires a person and throws them into a job. We try to blend personalities. We try to find the right person for the right job. It may take a little longer, but it makes us a stronger company.

I remember I had interviewed a girl who worked for the Ringling Bros. and Barnum & Bailey Circus. She had been a trapeze artist. Imagine the training, the discipline, the effort that goes into that. I wanted to hire her as a secretary. I went to Ted and said, "I've found this great girl to be the secretary for Bob Fields, one of our sales managers, but she has been with the circus, and I don't want to do anything that will tarnish AIM's reputation."

Ted said, "Goodness, why are you even asking me? She sounds like a prize."

And she was. Truth is, trapeze artists do not always fly through the air with the greatest of ease. On occasion they fall, and suffer permanent harm. They live with pain and are not likely to complain about the small aggravations that are part of working in most offices.

As part of her act, she jumped off the platform and into a large balloon filled with air. Well, one night in California the generator went out, and when she jumped all the air went out of the balloon and she hit the floor hard. Both of her legs and ankles were broken badly, one leg was shattered, and she had multiple surgeries.

She didn't withdraw into a shell. She had a great personality. Her childhood had been very difficult, which is why she went away to the circus. Now she was married and had a child and you could see how important her family was to her. So I felt she just fit our profile.

She retired about five years later to be a stay-at-home mom. She didn't leave us to go to another company. We enjoyed working with her, and when the circus came into town she always got AIM employees the prime seats.

Dale Griffin, Barrett Sides, and Steve Cao of
AIM's Asian portfolio management team.

Back then, that was a nice perk for the employees, taking your kids to the circus and sitting where you could see it all.

This is just one example of AIM's respect for diversity in our employee population. We love bright, competent, moderately aggressive self-starters, and that's what's made AIM so successful. I owe so much to Ted Bauer, Bob Graham and Gary Crum. I'm proud to have been part of AIM's tremendous success story.

JOEL DOBBERPUHL
SENIOR PORTFOLIO MANAGER — AIM VALUE FUND

I interviewed with portfolio managers Jon Schoolar and Lanny Sachnowitz about 10 years ago. One of the stock picks I gave them was Harnishfeger. I thought I laid out a compelling case. Later I found out from Jon they felt sorry for me for picking such a sad stock. Harnishfeger, by the way, was bought out last year for about the same market cap it had in 1990.

My main function the first year was to get lunch for Lanny and Craig Smith. I tried to be creative with events like "Pizza Week." My job got more difficult when Lanny

Clas Olsson, Jason Holzer, and Ben Hock. Olsson and Holzer are members of AIM's European portfolio management team. Hock is AIM's senior investment officer. All three managers are members of AIM's global growth team.

got on his health kick. Pizza with no cheese, burgers with no meat…well, you get the idea.

There was a certain austerity to the place when Jon was in charge. Come to think of it, that's probably why he hired Bob Kippes – he knew he would fit right in. Bob proved to be my lunch soul mate. We walked to Burger King for lunch one day, and he shared my excitement when the mini Taco Bell opened at Stop N Go. He was the very first customer and still has his receipt.

That second year when we both leapt over a 25k salary, I tried to get Bob to step it up with a $5 lunch at Goode Company, but he just couldn't do it. I guess he blew it all on the famous white pick-up. Bob responded to one of those lost-leader advertisements in the paper where it says "New trucks, from $4,999!" There was one, with no radio and no bumper. I think it was in Brenham. That was the only time I remember him coming in late.

Someone on the desk had to work with Dave on what was then AIM Strategic Income Fund. Lanny apparently didn't feel his lunch orders were enough torture, so I became the next sucker. When EMC was trading at $25, Dave would give me an order to short 1,000 shares at $50. I remember thinking to myself, "Surely, Dave, you could call me from the health club sometime between $25 and $50!" By the way, the stocks always made it to Dave's prices. The behavioral psychologist who proved the pain of losing is three times greater than the joy of winning conducted his study by making bets with Dave.

My big break came in 1992 when Claude Cody and I inherited AIM Value Fund. My only regret is we couldn't benefit from Claude's calendar skills since there was no calendar back then.

AIM is now a member of the AMVESCAP Group, and someday even AMVESCAP might be under a bigger umbrella. To me, AIM is Ted Bauer, Bob Graham, Gary Crum, and, depending on what day it is, Mike Cemo. I appreciate the stability of the management team, the emphasis they put on people and fairness, the freedom they have given us to make decisions, and the way they balance the interests of fund shareholders and company shareholders.

No place is perfect. There will always be policies or strategies you don't agree with. Headhunters will occasionally call and remind you that you can probably double your salary on the free-agent market.

But there must be more right than wrong, since so many of us are still around. What surprises me the most, 10 years later, is how much AIM remains a place of growth and opportunity. To those of you new to AIM, I am optimistic you will say 10 years from now and realize, as I did, that I came to the right place at the right time.

Ronnie Stein, Kevin Cronin, and Scott Pierce of AIM's trading department. Stein is manager of equity trading, Cronin is AIM's head of NYSE trading, and Pierce is AIM's head of NASDAQ trading.

CAROL DRAWE
SUPERVISOR OF INVESTMENT ADMINISTRATION

I applied for a job at AIM by responding to a classified ad. After a few weeks, I got a call from Judy Creel, who told me that the position had been filled. It was actually the head of the mailroom. But they had been intrigued by my resume and wanted to talk to me about an opening as the first secretary and support person in the Investment Department. Up until that time, Pat Hamill May, who was Mr. Bauer's secretary, had taken care of the correspondence and any large presentations, and the portfolio managers had handled all the other little details around the office.

Judy Creel was the one who sold me on the company. I liked the fact that she had been given a real opportunity and had done well with it. I liked the way she described the company. I had been a librarian earlier in my professional career, and left the interview with an armload of brochures and prospectuses. I asked for all the literature they had and I went home and read it. When they called to tell me I got the job I was excited, and a little scared, too.

I knew nothing about the mutual fund business. I'd never even seen a word processor in my entire life. I didn't have a clue as to what they were going to expect of me. I had a few friends who were sure I wouldn't last. One in particular calls from time to time and says, "Oh, you're still there!"

There was truly this family atmosphere. Everybody worked on everything. I was doing things for the legal department. We did some marketing. We graduated into the different phases of doing a presentation, the graphics, the typing, the copying and binding. We started a database. It was just so varied, with long hours and a lot of frustration because I had so much learning to do. But there was never a dull day and there still isn't. This is because the people who head the company were very impressive and very forgiving.

I think of this every time I get on an elevator and watch somebody press a button. My first week at AIM, I was in the elevator alone, going down to lunch, or whatever, and the three founders came running out to the lobby and yelled, "Hold the elevator!" In my haste, I pressed the "close door" button and the door shut in their faces. As I rode down to the lobby, alone, I was thinking, "Okay, Carol, you had three good days here. It was fun while it lasted."

But no one ever said a word. They were so forgiving, they probably didn't give it a thought. It was a fun first week and we reached a milestone, $4 billion in assets, I think, and Mr. Bauer had all of us to his house that Friday night for a party. Judy had gone to the great trouble of making beautiful nametags for everybody and putting on them what employee number they were, and the assets under management when you were hired. It really made everybody feel a part of this whole endeavor and indelibly fixed in my brain that I was Employee Number 60.

Once a week some of us in the investment department arrived at the office at 7 a.m. for a class that Dave Barnard taught on the various aspects of investing in mutual funds. It was one more opportunity to learn. It was a little fast for those of us who had no background in it, but most of my learning was by osmosis. Early on, I knew that I needed to keep all 20 of my ears open to what the portfolio managers and traders were doing. And I did, even while I was covering the phone or whatever else I was doing.

I tell the people who come to work in my group to pay attention and ask questions. A beautiful thing about most of the investment professionals is that they love to tell you about their job, what makes it work, what the problems are. They are perfectly willing to share.

One day, one of my brand new people said to me, "Oh, something is happening out there in the market." I said, "Oh, really, what?" She said, "It has to do with McDonald's." I said, "Oh," and asked her a few more questions and she didn't really have the answers.

As I was passing the portfolio managers later, I said, "What's going on with McDonald's today?" They looked at one another with puzzlement and one of them said, "I don't know. But we did send out for six orders of lunch at McDonald's."

Dick Berry, Franklin Ruben, Steve Turman, and Sharon Copper comprise AIM's tax-free bond team.

DALE GRIFFIN
SENIOR PORTFOLIO MANAGER –
CO-FOUNDER AIM INTERNATIONAL EQUITY DEPARTMENT

I came to AIM in September of 1989 to become the portfolio manager of a soon-to-be-launched fund called the AIM Prime Rate Premium Income Fund. Basically it would be a closed-end fund that would invest in the bank debt piece of leveraged buyout (LBO) recapitalizations. I came from Citibank where I had gained experience in corporate finance. What I didn't know at the time was that someone who had previously accepted the position had backed out and AIM was very anxious to fill the spot as it was time to finish the prospectus and start marketing the fund.

Bob Alley, Carolyn Gibbs, and Jan Friedli comprise
AIM's high-yield fixed-income management team.

Gary Crum got my name from a Citibank colleague
and called me. I didn't know Gary and, for that matter, I
had never heard of AIM. The exact date of Gary's call
escapes me, but I was just about to leave for a week-long
vacation in Vermont followed by another week of an
internal Citibank conference in Florida. After talking
awhile, Gary suggested I come by AIM's office to talk
about the open position. I asked if it could wait a couple
of weeks until I returned from my trip, but Gary was persistent so I agreed to come over the next day to meet with
some of the senior AIM executives.

My interview process basically consisted of a very
long lunch at Rao's – now called Los Andes – across the
street from AIM's office with Ted Bauer, Bob Graham,
Gary Crum, Mike Cemo, and Abbott Sprague. Then after
lunch I visited one-on-one with Ted and Gary. I also
spent some time with Bill Hoppe who had worked at
Citibank in Houston with me and had joined AIM about
a year earlier.

I was very impressed with everything and everyone I
saw. Although I didn't know much about the mutual fund
business, it was obviously growing very fast, and AIM
seemed to be on the cusp of a growth breakout.

The entrepreneurial spirit of a small company was infectious. Before leaving, Gary asked me where I could be reached in Vermont, so I gave him the name of the small inn where my wife, Ann, and I were going to stay. Later that night I spent about two hours on the phone with Bill Hoppe to try and get a feel for the company, where it was going, the culture, the senior people, and so forth. Without that conversation, I would never have been able to make the ultimate decision that I did.

About two days later, Ann and I were sitting outside in the backyard of the Buttercup Inn in Stowe, Vermont, when the owner came outside and said I had a phone call in the kitchen – the individual rooms didn't have phones. It was Gary and he offered me the job. Trying to be very nonchalant, I asked Gary if I could think about it for a day and call back. Of course, I had been thinking about nothing else since we had met.

Citibank had treated me very well and I could have easily made a good long career there, but after talking it over with Ann, I had already decided that if I got a good offer I would take it. Well, the offer was very good and included equity in the company. It certainly was a risk joining a small company, but it just felt right, so I accepted.

A couple of weeks later, while on the final day of our roadshow – ominously it was Friday, October 13th – the United Airlines LBO blew up, the stock market crashed. It was the beginning of the end of the crazy days of Drexel Burnham Lambert and the LBO hysteria, which had reached the frothy levels much like we saw in the Internet arena late 1999-early 2000. We then had to cancel the launch of the Prime Rate Fund.

At the time, it certainly seemed that my gamble to join AIM had come up snake eyes. However, what followed for me personally kind of sums up what AIM has always been about, which is an embodiment of the founders' core beliefs – people are your most important asset.

AIM could have given me a little severance and sent me packing, but they didn't. Instead, Ted and Gary told me that they would find something meaningful for me to do. In the back of my mind, I was thinking it was a good thing my resume was just updated, but they were true to their word. Because the junk-bond market was in disarray, and I had an analytical background, they asked me to work on our High Yield Fund with Polly Ahrendts and Stuart Coco. It was a difficult period in the market, but we waded through it.

Then one day in early 1991, Gary called me in his office. Ted was already there with a stern look on his face and I thought to myself that this was it – I just didn't know what "it" was.

Ted looked me in the eye and said that AIM wanted to launch an International Equity Fund and that if I could figure out how to do it, I could manage it. I was blown away. Now I am the senior member of our International Team of eight portfolio managers and analysts and we manage approximately $10 billion of international, global and regional funds.

In the end, the collapse of the Prime Rate Fund turned out to be one of the best things that ever happened to me in my life, even though it sure didn't seem so at the time. None of it would have happened, however, if AIM didn't believe in and take chances on relatively young people who are allowed a lot of individual responsibility and autonomy, with appropriate – but limited – oversight.

Karen Dunn Kelley, Scot Johnson, and Laurie Brignac comprise AIM's U.S. government fixed-income management team. Kelley and Brignac also are members of AIM's money market management team.

I know that someday when I'm reflecting back on my life from my rocking chair, the time and experiences that I have had at AIM, will bring back lots of great memories.

DAWN HAWLEY
CHIEF FINANCIAL OFFICER

The year AIM was founded, I graduated from college and was living in a suburb of Buffalo, New York. I earned an MBA in accounting and spent eight years in operations with Occidental Chemical, owned by Amoco Oil. In 1984, I moved with my husband to Houston, even as Occidental was transferring staff from its Houston offices to – Where else? – Niagara Falls.

I had been in cost accounting, budgeting, financial analysis, that sort of thing. When we moved, I got a job with a drilling company. I was one of the lucky ones. I was their assistant controller within three years. I had been contacted by a headhunter, and I was interested in Vista Chemicals, one of the companies started by an entrepreneur named Gordon Cane.

Michael Marek, Marques Mercier, Lyman Missimer III, Eric Lane,
Marcel Theriot, Colleen Ziegler, Dineen Hughes, and Esther Munoz
of AIM's money market management team. Also pictured at lower right is
Eric Peyton, an equity portfolio manager specializing in convertible securities.

I told this headhunter, "Look, if you can get me a job with one of the Cane companies, I will take a pay cut, because I'm looking for a place with a future." He kept calling me, saying that he was trying but jobs were really tight, the pay was really low. Then one day, he said, "I went and cold-called a new company called AIM." He

spelled it out, A-I-M. He said that the treasurer was looking for a budget person. He thought my background was
a fit. I said, "Well, what do I have to lose?"

This was July 1987. I came in and interviewed with a
man named Harold McElraft. The company was small,
125 people. They were looking at building some sort of
infrastructure and they understood their costs and needed a
budget. Then I interviewed with Ted Bauer, then Bob
Graham. They hired me within a month.

I was happy to leave the drilling business because it
was run by engineers, and I looked at this as an opportunity to join a company run by financial people. Not
accountants, but in a business that I could understand
better. I didn't know how to drill a well or put up a rig.
But I thought I could understand mutual funds.

This was a new position with no job description. They
really didn't have any job descriptions at the time, so they
were trying to build some structure. This is the funny
part. I started on October 5, 1987, a Monday. When I got
to the office, I asked for my boss, Harold, and he wasn't
there. He had quit. Two weeks later, the market dropped
508 points in one day. Ted went around and told people
not to worry about their jobs.

I had been working for 11 years, and I had never heard
the management of a company do or say anything like
that. Again, I went home and told my husband, "You're
not going to believe how this company reacts." Plus, we
were lean and mean. Look at our offices even now. It isn't
like we have gold-plated handles on the doors. I mean,
we have nice offices. I love them. But it isn't as if we were
awash in luxury.

There was no panic. They had really started to push the retail business and everything that was happening at AIM was new. They had to make a big investment at that time and the cost situation was becoming even more important. Again, we were small. Eventually, they hired a new controller and we put in a new budget system, so it was not an unusual way to start. You don't add 10 people until you decide what jobs need to be filled.

At AIM, you are valued so much more as to your background, and what you do for the company – big fish, small pond. You hear the word integrity used a lot around here, but it is the foundation of this company. This industry is built on compliance; it's sort of our No. 1 claim to fame. AIM always has been more people-oriented than the giant companies. Now as we get bigger it is harder to manage. But that is still the basic philosophy around here. As Ted says, "People are the product," and he means it.

From a strategic standpoint, when we negotiated with CIGNA, and ING and then INVESCO, one of the issues was autonomy. Ted, Bob, and Gary had to be the masters of our destinies, with the final say over what happens to this company. Anything else was unacceptable. And I have to say, that was a different attitude from the other companies in my background, where someone might say, "Yeah, you did a great job. But guess what? You won't have one tomorrow."

I have been in the workplace since 1976, so I haven't seen it all. I'm not a child of the Depression, either. But I have been in companies where you were promised a pay raise, only to be told that a wage freeze had gone into effect; where there is no such thing as a bonus, and they canceled the Christmas party, if not Christmas itself. And you have to be darned sure you turned off all the lights when you walked out the door.

Bob Graham runs the company now, and I remember talking to him about what the problems would be if we doubled in size. Bob said, "It's our job to keep this spirit alive, and to make sure that people understand that we are going to continue the traditions that Ted started. Sometimes it gets harder, but if you try, you can do it."

We believe that. We believe the best is yet to come.

DAVID HESSEL
DIRECTOR OF FINANCE

I was working with a lot of other people on the recapitalization of AIM in 1993. There was a big debt offering associated with that recapitalization and in conjunction that that deal, there were a number of us who had to go to New York and be at the closing. Ted Bauer and a lot of other people were there. Once the deal was completed, Dawn Hawley, Ted and I all ended up in the same cab on our way to the airport since we were all going to be on the same flight back to Houston.

Dawn and Ted had the foresight not to check any baggage, but I ended up checking a bag for some reason. Dawn and Ted were nice enough to wait for me to get my bag out of the baggage claim. At the time, it was embarrassing to have someone of Ted's stature to wait for someone like me to get my bags, which I shouldn't have checked in the first place. Many other corporate executives would have cut and run, but Ted was very patient and gracious.

The moral of this story? I no longer check baggage for a one- or two-day trip.

*Ron Sloan, Derek Izuel, Roger Mortimer, and Michael Yellen
manage equity funds out of AIM's San Francisco office.
Sloan specializes in mid-cap stocks, Izuel in global resource stocks,
and Mortimer and Yellen in health-care stocks.*

JEFF HORNE
ASSISTANT TO THE PRESIDENT

I joined AIM's Legal and Compliance team in the spring of 1988. During my first week, I made a rather egregious error in judgment involving one Charles T. Bauer. After Mr. Bauer informed me of my error in vivid detail, I thought it best to inform my supervisor that it may not be worth my while to unpack my newly delivered box of office supplies.

After hearing my tale, my supervisor gave, what I thought to be at the time, a rather unconvincing "It will be OK" speech. Here it is 12 years later and I am still with AIM, because the speech I had heard that day wasn't a speech at all – it was AIM's philosophy – "Our people are our product."

AIM realizes that mistakes are a part of learning, and AIM not only urges its employees to set high standards and goals, but actually provides the tools and the understanding necessary for its employees to reach their full potential. You would be hard pressed to find another company that cares so much about its employees.

MARK McMEANS
PRESIDENT — AIM PRIVATE ASSET MANAGEMENT

I actually started out as an auditor at Peat Marwick back in late '86. I had one week of orientation and then I was assigned to AIM. I had never heard of AIM. I had heard of the toothpaste, but never the mutual fund company.

AIM had bought the rights to manage the Weingarten, Charter, and Constellation Funds several months before. Peat Marwick was the auditor of AIM and its subsidiaries and most of its funds with only a couple of exceptions. Being an auditor is a pretty miserable experience inherently, but the good thing is that you get to go to a company like AIM and meet its people and learn about what they do. And then you rotate off and go to American Capital for a couple months of the year and then to Criterion for a couple months of the year. The good thing about it is that you get to go to all these different firms, meet the players, and see what all these businesses are like.

I first started trying to join AIM in '89, the rationale being that the firm was much smaller than anybody else, but very entrepreneurial, very dynamic. The owners of the company were the management and were here every day. They hired a lot of young people, a lot of go-getters, and the atmosphere was very different here than it was at any of the other local competitors. And being from Texas, quite frankly, it's neat to be in this industry and get to live here as opposed to living in New York or Boston.

I first tried to work here in '89 and was unsuccessful. I talked to most anybody that I knew that would listen and decided to go back to school. I went to Texas Commerce first, worked in the trust department, did that for a while, and then was just lucky.

I had been rejected I don't know how many times for work here and had taken a job with Citicorp while I was still in school and read in the paper that AIM had bought the CIGNA funds, back in the spring of '92. So I just sat down and wrote Ted Bauer a letter. He didn't know me from the man in the moon.

I wrote, "Congratulations on your acquisition," and "When do I start? I finish school in the next six weeks." It was a difficult time for us; when you sign up to do a deal like Citicorp, you go to New York for a six- or seven-month training program. My wife was pregnant with our first and she had a career. And this was a real blessing for us in our life, as everything just fell into place.

I started to work for Abbott Sprague. He was looking for someone with an accounting background, who worked in a trust department and had gone back to school.

I remember in late '92 when we had about $18 billion under management. Ted was very visible when we were all on one or two floors. Bill Hoppe and I were talking and Ted came in and said something to the effect of that at the end of the decade we wanted to have $100 billion in assets under management.

"You either going to be a boutique player, or you are going to be a scale player," he said. We wouldn't be able to

Marilyn Miller, Mary Kay Coleman, Glenda Dayton,
Norman Woodson, Margaret Vinson, and Gary Wendler of
AIM's Retail Marketing Department. Miller is director of marketing,
Coleman is manager of marketing communications, Dayton is director
of product management, Woodson is manager of communication resources,
Vinson is manager of electronic commerce, and
Wendler is manager of marketing research and analysis.

survive in the mid-tier range. I remember Ted leaving the office and Bill Hoppe and I saying to each other, "How in the world are we ever going to get $100 billion under management?" At the time it was a profound statement.

It was really fun when everybody was on one floor and everybody knew everybody else. But some things haven't changed which is important.

One is the investment discipline which we talk about and we tout in our ads. But having not been on this floor for many years at the company and now being in equities I see that its something that is taken very seriously and its

Judy Creel, Brenda Thomas, Herman Kluge, Karla Siemens,
and Nancy Beck. Creel is director of corporate resources,
Thomas is manager of human resources, Kluge is manager of facilities,
Siemens is manager of meeting planning and travel, and
Beck is director of sponsorships and promotions.

something that we can almost take for granted because its inherent in what we do. Other firms don't necessarily have a discipline that makes sense that's tested over time. It has been probably the most important part of what we do.

The other things that are important are our conservative nature. There was an article in *The Wall Street Journal* today about how we didn't run some ads touting performance despite the market volatility. That's an example of how being conservative in our nature has really withstood the test of time.

It seems like the things that have made AIM a great place to work are all still in place – which is amazing given our growth rate, which is just been incredible and almost unprecedented in our industry. Those things are the strength of the environment, the culture, the leadership. People are left to their own devices. There is no manual with reams and reams of descriptions of policies and procedures. I mean, there's important structure where structure needs to take place, but we are so decentralized and entrepreneurial, even with 2,000-plus employees.

That's kept AIM a fun place to work. There's so much happening here. I think the leadership structure is pretty interesting. The natures and strengths of the three founders complement one another.

NANCY MARTIN
ASSISTANT LEGAL COUNSEL

I remember interviewing at AIM and being most concerned during the process about whether the company would make it in the long term. I was convinced by those I interviewed with that they very much understood the industry and were very interested in the people who worked there. I joined AIM in March of '87.

In October of '87, while I was attending the ICI Tax and Accounting Conference with Jackie Fogle and Dana Sutton, the market dropped significantly. I was further impressed about senior management's dedication to its employees when I was told that Ted was walking around the office reassuring people that their jobs were secure.

I have fond memories of midnight croquet at some of the "away" board meetings. I remember several good matches. In one match, Jack Caldwell was my partner and Ted Bauer and Gary Crum were our opponents. I could hardly see the wickets, yet somehow managed to make some extremely fortunate shots. Gary was always at the

Stuart Coco, Polly Ahrendts, Mark McMeans, Gary Beauchamp,
Kamala Sachidanandan, and Nick White. Coco is director of
fixed-income research, Ahrendts is director of equity research,
McMeans is president of AIM Private Asset Management,
Beauchamp is AIM's economic strategist, Sachidanandan is director
of marketing for AIM Private Asset Management, and
White is marketing liaison for AIM's Investment Department.

ready to "send me" when things got too close. He also
sent Jack's ball into some tall grass that took us a while to
locate. As usual, Ted and Gary won.

   I remember getting involved in an issue with Mary
Corcoran where one of our shareholders was suspected of
being involved in mail fraud. While Mary and I were
making every effort to cooperate with the U.S. Postal
Inspector, he was asking us to do something that would
violate the 1940 Act. We explained the problem, but he
threatened to have us both arrested and jailed over the
Thanksgiving weekend for contempt if we did not comply with his request. We were able to work out a solution

that was satisfactory to both of us...thank goodness!

I remember being involved in a suit filed by a share-holder after the 1987 market decline. The case never went to trial, but we went through fairly extensive discovery and ended up in mediation. The deposition phase was very unpleasant – and I thought that was true for both sides. I was shocked after we finally reached a settlement that the former shareholder invited me to stop by and visit should I ever be in his neighborhood.

Finally, I have many memories of our CIGNA deal. I remember Bill Kleh and I making a call to the CIGNA lawyers. We were deep in negotiation on an issue and Bill was upset. We couldn't reach the CIGNA lawyers, so we attempted to call outside counsel. While we were on hold waiting to speak with the lawyer, Bill expressed his displeasure with some of the folks at CIGNA and how they were working the deal.

We then heard a recorded message that stunned us both. We had not disconnected from the first call to CIGNA, but had accidentally conferenced in their voice mail. All of Bill's remarks were on their voicemail!

The only thing I could think to do was to call one of the other lawyers at CIGNA that I had worked with, put on my best Scarlett O'Hara impression, and suggest that Bill had made some unfortunate comments in frustration and that if they were gentlemen, they would not listen to the message, but would delete it since it was not intended for them to hear.

PAT HAMILL MAY
ADMINISTRATIVE SUPPORT MANAGER

I was referred to AIM by M. David Lowe in 1980 when Ted Bauer needed a secretary. I sat on the sofa in the same office he has today, and he sat in a chair. At the end of the interview, he said, "Well, do you want the job?"

I looked at him and gulped and thought, "This is a man that you don't say 'if' or 'maybe' or 'I'll have to get back to you.'" And I said, "Yes, I do." I had no specific idea what the salary was. His former secretary had taken a maternity leave, and he had been using an office temp for a number of months. I knew nothing about the business, but this didn't seem to trouble him. He put you at ease right away. There were fewer than 20 people in the company and it was the best decision I ever made in my life. I didn't know enough to be scared.

In my first year or two, we were still small, but growing steadily. I would work with Gary Crum and Bob Graham and Ted and Steve Pouns, who was our financial analyst, one of the original group, who is no longer here. We would often work late into the evenings. One night, I was at my desk and I was getting ready to meet someone at a restaurant. It was around 6:30 and I had taken my shoes off because my feet hurt. I was about to leave and went to put my shoes on and I couldn't find them.

I had been working hard, we all had, and I was tired, but I hunted everywhere for those shoes. I couldn't find them. I asked Bob. I asked Gary. I asked Ted. No one had seen them. Well, they carried it on to the point where I was nearly in tears. I could walk out of the building in my stocking feet, fine. I could walk to the car, fine. But I couldn't walk into Rudi's Restaurant without any shoes!

They had hidden them in the file cabinet. Of course, it would never have occurred to me to look in the file cabinet for my shoes. And it was an important date for me, and I was furious with them. I've forgotten who confessed.

AIM veterans know where to find Ted Bauer whenever the company's annual Holiday Gala is held at The Houston Museum of Natural Science. Bauer, whose nickname is "Bones," says he appropriately stations himself near the dinosaur exhibit.

Ted was always rightfully concerned about how we spent our money. He did not hire people needlessly because if you had a downturn he did not want to lay off anyone. He was frugal in those ways. So he came to my desk one morning and asked where we were going to have the Christmas party. I said we'd picked the Doubletree, but I hadn't put down the deposit.

He said he thought maybe we could have it here and save all that expense. We had just taken over the rest of the floor and at that point it was pretty vacant. I thought

John Deane, Paul Wise, Carol Relihan, Dawn Hawley, Tim Cox, and Dan Brennan. Deane is president of information technology, Wise is vice president of information technology, Relihan is chief legal counsel, Hawley is chief financial officer, Cox is director of compliance, and Brennan is director of risk management.

we could pull it off. But I knew that initially people would be disappointed. If a party has become a real social event, and you move it back into your offices, the impression is that you are scaling way back. But I'm a very positive person and I kept talking it up, telling people to just wait and see.

I sealed off the double doors that were back there and announced from then on nobody was allowed in that area. I arranged with Maxim's to cut us a good deal on the hors d'oeuvres, and I hired a pianist with a portable keyboard to provide the music. I went around to all the perimeter offices and put in 25-watt bulbs so that the lighting was dim. I had candles everywhere, balloons, good food, good music and it worked out beautifully. And it cost us less money!

I eventually made the move to Retail Marketing and have remained in that department in a number of positions. I have a license to sell mutual funds and a license to supervise people. When I made the move, I had to be licensed in six to eight weeks. So I did all of my studying on my own and the company paid for me to attend a three-day seminar.

Having worked for Ted, I felt a lot of pressure to pass the licensing test. I went to the examining area in a building on Richmond, and the test took nearly two hours to complete. You knew immediately if you passed, and I did with fairly good marks. I called Ted from a pay phone and said, "Well, I passed."

And he said, "I know that."

I said, "How could you possibly know?'

And Ted said, 'If you hadn't passed, you wouldn't have called me."

FRANNIE REED
SECRETARY TO THE PRESIDENT AND CEO

I think I had been at AIM for about four years when Judy Creel told me she almost didn't hire me. She thought I was going to go back to Maine. But soon I hope to observe my 20th anniversary here.

When I first came here, we used to take the telephone list and reduce it and stick it on the telephone. That's how small we were! I think I was the 24th person to come here. I worked for years trying to keep the telephone list on one page. I tried everything, even reducing the font. But look at it now. It fits in a notebook!

Jim Stueve, Gene Needles, Mike Vessels, Joe Seymour, Mark Santero, John Cooper, Stephen Bitteker, Gary Littlepage, and Pat Hamill May. Stueve, Needles, and Vessels are national sales managers of AIM's IIDD, NYSE, and FID Retail Marketing Divisions, respectively. Seymour is national sales manager of retirement plans, Santero is national sales manager of AIM's Institutional Marketing Division, and Cooper is director of retirement plans. Bitteker is director of offshore fund sales, Littlepage is manager of project and product development, and May is manager of administrative staff for retail marketing.

In 1981, we had one corporate accountant who was also secretary to the treasurer. We had only one fund accountant – Kamellia Ishak. She still works here. And we had four shareholder services people. Four! Now we have them on that many floors!

I keep a list of every employee who's ever worked here, even if they've been terminated. I have pictures of everybody. It goes from Mr. Bauer through the last employee who was hired.

Right before we started the company 401(k) plan, probably back in '84 or '85, I remember Mr. Bauer standing outside his door and he was telling us about this great plan. At that time, I knew absolutely nothing about saving for retirement. I mean, I had a little savings account. I can remember him saying, "You've got to put into this because, Frannie, you are going to be my age before you know it."

Now, I think I am one year younger than he was when he said that. And now I could retire…it's just unreal! It just grows and grows and grows. At first you see maybe $10,000 and you are just like "Whoa!" It's like a snowball rolling down a hill, the way it picks up momentum.

I was 44 when I started at AIM. And you would think that at 44, you don't have that much time to save for retirement. But boy you really do, if you put your mind to it.

After Mr. Bauer told me and I saw how it worked, I went home and said "Okay, kids, this is what I want you to do, even if it's just $25 dollars a month. You could blow that on anything, but if you just put it away, it just grows and grows." My retirement will be completely different now than if I hadn't worked at AIM. I thank God every day.

CAROL RELIHAN
CHIEF LEGAL COUNSEL

My first introduction to AIM was when I was an associate at Ballard Spahr's Denver office. Bill Kleh, who was a partner there at the time, asked me if I'd like to work on a mutual fund acquisition with him. It turned out to be AIM's acquisition of the Charter Fund from Julian Lerner.

The first time I came here was in the winter, and I was wearing a wool suit. When I got off the plane in Houston, I thought I had stepped into a sauna. I enjoyed working on the deal, which gave me a chance to meet Bob Graham, Ted Bauer, Harold McElraft, Alex Ciccone, Stan Griffith, and some of the other folks here at the time.

A few months later, Bill had joined AIM as general counsel. Shortly after he did so, he needed another lawyer on his staff. When he called me, Denver was going through tough economic times, and many of the securities firms were closing their Denver offices. It was looking like time to learn bankruptcy law and switch from corporate and securities. I interviewed at AIM. Ted Bauer said, "I think we can offer you steady work." He certainly kept that promise!

I am very grateful to have had an opportunity to participate in the kind of success that AIM has had over the years. This firm has grown because people cared about what they do and cared about each other. So many people have consistently pitched in to any effort that was necessary, behaved in a highly professional way, and tried their best to achieve good results for our clients.

Ted Bauer is one of my heroes. He built an inspiring American success story from almost nothing. It's always been fun to be part of the growth and part of making good things happen.

Tony Green, Laura Slowensky, Linda Warriner, Sidney Dilgren, and Ira Cohen. Green is president of AIM Fund Services, Slowensky is manager of client services, Warriner is manager of client services in Austin, Dilgren is manager of AIM's Control Department and AIM Institutional Fund Services, and Cohen is manager of brokerage operations and commissions.

DANA SUTTON
TREASURER

Ever since I've been at AIM, things have never slowed down. It's a tight-knit group, very friendly, and eager to make you feel you belong. To some extent, as an accountant your job doesn't change. You just add more zeroes. I started as a fund accountant. At the time, all the accounting was done by a custodian bank. What AIM was looking to do was expand the department, bring the accounting and the supervision in house.

Things worked out and I was made the supervisor they promised I would be. There were two other fund accountants besides myself, and 50 or more funds. We get

Left to right, David Hessel, Dana Sutton and John Arthur were key number-crunchers for AIM during the 1990s. Hessel and Sutton recently were promoted to director of finance and treasurer, respectively, after Arthur retired as treasurer.

involved in special projects and set the dividends for the fund. We do all that, plus chair a valuation committee that sets the policy and procedures that the funds follow. If the trading is stopped on the exchanges, the committee will determine what the price is at the close of business.

Calculating net asset values (NAVs) can be very stressful. We get different groups involved. Then, we have to meet a time deadline to get the price in the paper every morning. Occasionally, you'll see people running.

When I found out I was pregnant with my daughter Megan, Mr. Bauer offered me the crib of his son, Douglas. When he brought it down from the attic, or wherever, he found it had a little more wear and tear than he recalled. So he went out and bought a new one.

B.J. THOMPSON
RETAIL MARKETING SUPPORT MANAGER

I love to tell the story of how I joined AIM. My neighbor, Ted Bauer, walked down the street to share a glass of wine with my husband and me as was our custom to enjoy a couple of times a week at one house or another. Ted found me at the computer writing a proposal to my employer that would allow me to work out of my home, servicing the Houston accounts for which I was responsible. The company for which I worked 17½ years was closing its Houston office and relocating to Chicago.

A couple of weeks later, Mr. Bauer asked if I had received a response to my proposal. I replied, "No, they are old fashioned where women are concerned." He asked if he could call me for an interview, which he did, and the fun began. In its early days, AIM took an aggressive stance on hiring women for positions traditionally held by males. I recognize that AIM was a frontrunner in this area and, as a woman, share my appreciation.

MARGARET VINSON
DIRECTOR OF ELECTRONIC COMMERCE

Abbott Sprague hired me at AIM. Once hired, I found out why. Abbott thought that by asking people how much money they had in their checking account, it would show how detailed-oriented a person was. I answered with a 100 percent accuracy down to the penny. Abbott was apparently very impressed. What Abbott did not know, however, was how easy it is to balance your checkbook when the total equals $0.00. I guess he figured since I was the most desperate for money, I would be the most aggressive in the job.

In my first job here as an institutional services rep, Mr. Bauer stopped by every day to ask how the funds were doing. I always tell people I was born and raised at AIM. It was my first job out of college and have never had a reason to leave. With such incredible growth, there has always been a great opportunity for me to increase my skill set and keep myself challenged.

When all employees were on the 19th floor and half the floor was trading, set up with fixed-income, equity, and institutional marketing all together, a couple of people went through the trading floor and set all the phones to hold and speaker. We had surround sound Christmas music blaring through the floor. Very festive!

When AIM first created the IT help desk a memo was sent out saying "Anything you need to know, just ask." But they failed to specify technical questions. Brian O'Neill was the only help-desk person. On a regular basis, we called Brian to ask questions like "At what temperature do you cook a turkey? How many feet of wire is in the ceilings? How long of a drive is it to Miami?" It has always been possible to maintain a sense of humor at AIM.

Co-founders Bob Graham, Ted Bauer, and Gary Crum
close the book on a quarter century of AIM history.

APPENDIX

AIM HISTORY OF ASSETS UNDER MANAGEMENT
AND NUMBER OF EMPLOYEES   1976-2000*

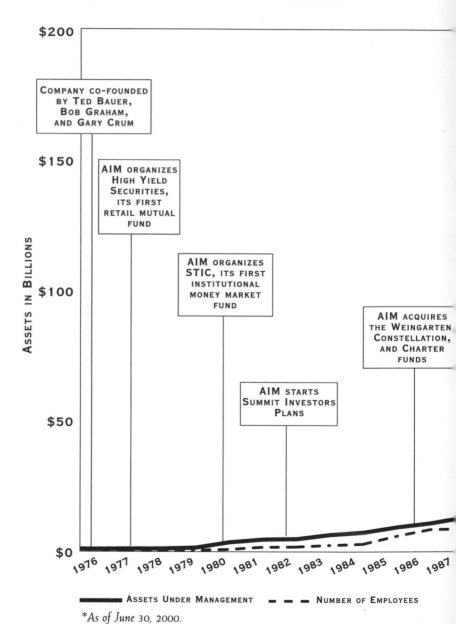

*As of June 30, 2000.

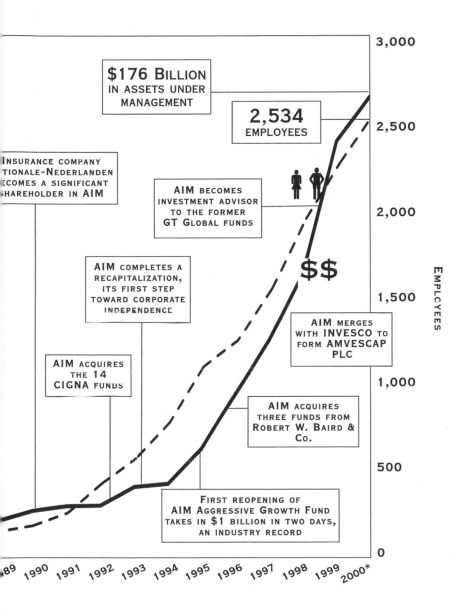

$176 BILLION IN ASSETS UNDER MANAGEMENT

2,534 EMPLOYEES

INSURANCE COMPANY [NA]TIONALE-NEDERLANDEN [B]ECOMES A SIGNIFICANT [S]HAREHOLDER IN AIM

AIM BECOMES INVESTMENT ADVISOR TO THE FORMER GT GLOBAL FUNDS

AIM COMPLETES A RECAPITALIZATION, ITS FIRST STEP TOWARD CORPORATE INDEPENDENCE

$$

AIM MERGES WITH INVESCO TO FORM AMVESCAP PLC

AIM ACQUIRES THE 14 CIGNA FUNDS

AIM ACQUIRES THREE FUNDS FROM ROBERT W. BAIRD & CO.

FIRST REOPENING OF AIM AGGRESSIVE GROWTH FUND TAKES IN $1 BILLION IN TWO DAYS, AN INDUSTRY RECORD

3,000
2,500
2,000
1,500
1,000
500
0

EMPLOYEES

'89 1990 1991 1992 1993 1994 1995 1996 1997 1998 1999 2000*

AIM MISSION STATEMENT

Our mission is to be a premier

investment management company,

helping investors reach their financial goals

by providing them with

investment products and services

through financial intermediaries.

We will pursue our mission by

delivering superior investment performance,

marketing, and service, and by

serving the interests of our clients,

employees, and business partners.

PRINCIPLES OF SUCCESS

Surpass Expectations

Long-term growth and success demand that we provide performance and service that surpasses our customers' expectations.

Unquestioned Integrity

We are mindful of the trust we ask our customers to place in us and will continuously earn that trust by conducting our business in accordance with the highest legal and ethical standards.

Customer Focus

Our success is driven by satisfying our customers' needs and is dependent on our ability to adapt to a changing marketplace and continuously deliver products and services that offer them true value.

Community Involvement

We strive to be a good corporate citizen of the communities in which we live and work, encouraging participation in and support of community activities by AIM and its employees.

Entrepreneurial Environment

We seek to provide an environment that attracts talented, energetic and creative people who work well together. We believe such people flourish in an environment that encourages initiative and innovation.

Shared Commitment

Our most valuable assets are our reputation and our people. We strive to create a culture in which everyone can share responsibility for and participate in AIM's success.

Sustained Growth

We strive to profitably grow and expand AIM's business in order to provide increased opportunities for our customers, employees and business partners.

AIM CORPORATE VISION

AIM will be a leading investment manager for individuals and organizations worldwide. Our products will be marketed globally with our strategic partners, including other units of AMVESCAP, with whom we will capitalize on investment management and distribution opportunities. We will also leverage our extensive network of financial intermediaries, with whom we maintain mutually profitable, long-term relationships.

Our broad product line will include options to help all individual and institutional investors achieve their financial goals – making millions of investors glad that they invested with AIM. We will manage traditional investment products, as well as develop innovative new products to meet our client's needs.

AIM will be known as a model organization in terms of its work environment, industry leadership and community involvement. Employees will be viewed as long-term assets and AIM will foster an entrepreneurial culture characterized by highly competitive incentives, and individual and team accountability for success. Customer priorities will drive our business, and our customer service will rank among the best in the industry.

Our investment performance will reflect our goals of asset preservation, combined with elements of top-ranked performance. Overall, AIM's performance will consistently rank in top half and, on selected products with more high-performance goals, top quartile. Technology will keep us competitive and effective in the workplace. AIM will continue to grow at a sustained rate and our financial performance will be highly ranked within our industry.

IN SHORT, WE WILL BE RECOGNIZED AS THE PREMIER INVESTMENT FIRM AND THE TOP CHOICE AS THE PLACE TO WORK BY THE BEST AND THE BRIGHTEST IN OUR INDUSTRY.

AIM CODE OF ETHICS

AIM's fiduciary relationships and the success of our clients rely upon trust and commitment to our integrity and honesty. This Summary is intended to highlight and promote AIM's high standards of ethical conduct.

DOs

1. As an "Access Person" get permission from Code of Ethics Officer before you buy or sell a security

2. As an "Access Person" or a Registered Representative, confirm security trades within 10 days of execution

3. Give the Code of Ethics Officer a list of any new brokerage accounts you open (forms are available)

4. Read the Code. You must know and understand the following:
   - What is "Insider Trading"
   - Who is considered an "Insider"
   - What is considered:
     "Material Information"
     "Non-Public Information"
   - What are the penalties and fines for insider trading violations
   - What to do if you think you may have inside information

5. Comply with:
   - Federal regulations and state laws
   - AIM's Procedures and Guidelines

6. As a supervisor, oversee your employees to prevent any violations

7. Avoid conflicts of interest and strive to meet the highest ethical and fiduciary standards

8. Be diligent and thorough in investment recommendations and investment actions

9. Report securities holdings upon employment and annually

10. Attend the annual Code of Ethics Review

DON'Ts

1. Communicate material, non-public information or trade in securities for yourself or client accounts on this information

2. Acquire unregistered securities issued in private placements without written permission

3. Engage in a business activity that competes with AIM, unless you receive written permission

4. Influence for your benefit any investment strategy followed by AIM for client accounts

5. Disclose information regarding securities holdings or transactions of AIM clients or matters which AIM considers confidential

6. Acquire or dispose of beneficial ownership of a security based on your knowledge of transactions already completed, being taken or being considered by AIM

7. Solicit or accept from a broker/dealer or vendor certain gifts or gratuities

8. Purchase (by you or your immediate family) securities issued during an "initial public offering"

9. Cause (or influence) a client account to buy or sell a security you beneficially own, unless first disclosed to the Investment Policy Committee

10. Buy or sell, for yourself or client accounts, restricted list securities

11. Excessively trade securities short-term

12. Acquire beneficial ownership of corporate bonds held in a client account and rated less than investment grade

AIM
FUNDS®

AIM SENIORITY LIST—
TOP 100

Name	Hire Date	Name	Hire Date
Ted Bauer	8-4-76	B.J. Thompson	9-8-86
Gary Crum	9-21-76	Sidney Dilgren	10-13-86
Bob Graham	11-22-76	Carol Relihan	11-10-86
Judy Creel	7-1-79	Julie Yeargain	2-9-87
Abbott Sprague	2-11-80	Chuck Grob	2-17-87
Pat Hamill May	10-13-80	Nancy Martin	3-23-87
Kamellia Ishak	12-22-80	Gerilyn Edgar	6-3-87
Frannie Reed	8-17-81	Nadean Livings	6-29-87
Gary Beauchamp	8-31-81	Greg Stock	6-29-87
David Barnard	5-10-82	Esther Munoz	7-14-87
Dana Sutton	5-16-83	Lanny Sachnowitz	7-20-87
Eva Bencze	4-24-84	Donna Tolopka	7-20-87
Steve Turman	1-23-85	Joe Dichiara	7-24-87
Kathy Pflueger	2-25-85	Dick Berry	8-17-87
Mary Gentempo	4-1-85	Heather Lazare	8-20-87
Polly Ahrendts	7-8-85	Dawn Hawley	10-5-87
Mary Benson	8-12-85	Torri Evans	11-11-87
Betty Havard	8-26-85	Susan Van Dusen	12-17-87
Carol Drawe	10-1-85	Idania Reyes	1-11-88
Lisa Howie	2-20-86	Sharon Poessel	1-18-88
Michele Harrison	4-14-86	Doug O'Dell	2-1-88
Jodi Cook	5-12-86	Jeff Horne	2-8-88
Kathi Douglas	5-15-86	Kim McAuliffe	4-12-88
Jon Schoolar	8-25-86	Nina Smith	6-27-88
Jim Salners	9-8-86	Mike Cemo	8-29-88

Name	Hire Date	Name	Hire Date
Stuart Coco	8-29-88	Esther McManus	2-23-90
Bill Hoppe	9-12-88	John Frame	4-2-90
Patti Hefley	9-19-88	Larry Manierre	5-9-90
Brian Pierce	11-21-88	Judy Brown	5-14-90
David Hessel	11-28-88	Bob Cherichella	7-1-90
Bob Kippes	1-30-89	Bruce Simmons	7-2-90
Linda Rodriguez	2-14-89	Connie Ramirez	7-9-90
Michelle Gonzales	3-8-89	Julie Bell	7-23-90
Dineen Hughes	3-13-89	Mary Nell Schleinschok	7-24-90
Jose Melgar	5-15-89		
Brian O'Neill	5-16-89	Laura Thompson	7-31-90
Becky Flores	5-22-89	Donna Laroche	8-6-90
Karen Consley	5-30-89	Mark Carter	8-7-90
Neal Seidle	6-8-89	Ken Zschappel	8-7-90
Kim Gibson	6-13-89	Joel Dobberpuhl	8-20-90
Mary Ellen Moore	6-26-89	Pat Bray	9-17-90
Joan Kennedy	9-12-89	Rob Morris	10-15-90
Karen Dunn Kelley	9-18-89	Anne-Marie Mullen	10-29-90
Dale Griffin	9-28-89	Angela Mitchell	11-21-90
Margaret Vinson	10-23-89	Addie Townsend	1-3-91
Barrett Sides	1-30-90	Raymond Gayton	1-14-91
Gary Trappe	2-1-90	Anne Marie Fearnow	1-15-91
Gordon Sprague	2-12-90	Jason Gray	1-22-91
Sheri Morris	2-20-90	Meggan Walsh	1-22-91

As of July 5, 2000

A